TEACHING

FOR

THINKING

Edited by
James W. Keefe
Herbert J. Walberg

National Association of Secondary School Principals
1904 Association Drive ▪ Reston, Virginia 22091-1537
(703) 860-0200 - (800) 253-7746

About the Authors

Herbert J. Walberg is research professor of education, University of Illinois, Chicago.

Barbara Z. Presseisen is director of national networking, Research for Better Schools, Philadelphia, Pa.

Robert J. Marzano is director of research, Mid-Continent Regional Educational Laboratory, Aurora, Colo.

Francis Schrag is professor, Department of Educational Policy Studies, University of Wisconsin-Madison.

Barak Rosenshine is professor, Department of Educational Psychology, University of Illinois, Champaign.

Joseph Guenther is professor, Department of Social Sciences, Parkland College, and assistant professor, University of Illinois, Champaign.

Ann L. Brown is professor of math, science and technology education, and educational psychology, University of California, Berkeley.

Joseph C. Campione is professor, School of Education, University of California, Berkeley.

Charles A. Letteri is associate professor of educational psychology, University of Vermont, Burlington.

Robert H. Ennis is professor of philosophy of education, University of Illinois, Champaign.

Barry K. Beyer is professor of educational leadership and human development, George Mason University, Fairfax, Va.

Robert J. Sternberg is IBM professor of psychology and education, Yale University, New Haven, Conn.

James W. Keefe is director of research, National Association of Secondary School Principals, Reston, Va.

Copyright 1992, NASSP
ISBN 0-88210-265-6

Published by the National Association of Secondary School Principals
Executive Director: Timothy J. Dyer
Deputy Executive Director: Thomas F. Koerner
Associate Director of Publications: Carol A. Bruce
Technical Editor: Eugenia Cooper Potter
Senior Publications Specialist: Jody Guarino

CONTENTS

Teaching for thinking is both an ideal and a goal. As an ideal, it has been at the forefront of many educational reform efforts of the past century. As a goal, it has been an elusive destination, pursued more often by good intentions and impractical theories than by workable programs. Some of this is beginning to change.

In the past decade, philosophers, psychologists, and educational practitioners have all come to agree on the importance of effective thinking to success in school and in life. Creative models and programs have proliferated. A movement has materialized. We are now at the crest of a scholarly and public policy wave of approval for the efficacy of good thinking. Virtually everyone acknowledges the modern information explosion and proposes that we teach for effective thinking. The questions remain about who, what, when, and how.

The distinguished authors of this book propose some sensible answers to these questions. Not all questions are resolved, but the issues are laid out and clarified. A matrix is proposed for thinking about thinking.

We invite your thoughtful reading and reflection.

James W. Keefe
Director of Research, NASSP

Herbert J. Walberg

The three words in the title of this book are carefully chosen. In planning the volume, we intended to represent a variety of current efforts to incorporate thought-provoking methods into teaching. Our further hope was to convey contemporary ideas, approaches, and programs, in a set of crisply written chapters.

Many policy makers and educators believe that it is important to emphasize thinking in today's schools. The National Assessment of Educational Progress and other testing programs suggest that students have improved their rates of knowledge acquisition in the last decade. They are lagging, however, in the "higher thinking skills" such as analysis, synthesis, problem solving, and applications. Comparisons of U.S. students with those in other nations, moreover, show that they lag more on higher than lower order skills (Walberg, 1983, 1988).

None of this is to say that we can put knowledge aside. Facts and ideas go together; it is hard to find an expert thinker in any field who lacks knowledge. If we gave priority to thinking alone, then a course in logic or even a programmed computer might suffice—but they obviously do not. Students need knowledge to think about.

But neither can facts alone suffice. Thinking is important, even at the outset in acquiring new knowledge. Thought is required, for example, in deciding what knowledge to pursue. Psychological research suggests that student thoughtfulness promotes learning efficiency. Students benefit from explicit teaching about how to set their own learning goals and how to monitor their progress. Reflection about knowledge and ideas can lead to insights that improve long-term retention and problem solving.

How can such ideas be translated into curricula and instructional activities? The following overview provides capsule summaries and highlights of the chapters.

Overview

The chapters are divided into three sections: Curriculum Developments defines key curricular terms and offers a framework and general examples of teaching tactics. Teaching and Assessment describes new methods for teaching thinking and assessing the degree to which it has been accomplished. Concluding Perspectives synthesizes research and practical methods of teaching thinking and analyzes the contributions of this book. Some specific contributions of each chapter are as follows:

Curriculum Developments

Barbara Presseisen distinguishes thinking from thinking about thinking ("meta-cognition"), learners' awareness, and regulation of their thinking. She also describes "conation" (motivation and striving) and knowledge representation and shows how these ideas are being incorporated in curricula to promote thinking.

Robert Marzano begins with a conceptual framework and tactics for thinking. He divides 22 tactics into three domains—learning to learn, content thinking, and reasoning—which, as he illustrates, can be appropriately assigned to subjects at specific grade levels.

Francis Schrag argues that to teach thinking is to create a disposition rather than to impart a formula, and that deep thinking is specific to the subject matter. He describes several ways to promote such classroom thoughtfulness.

Teaching and Assessment

Barak Rosenshine and Joseph Guenther describe "scaffolding," temporary instructional supports for students to bridge the gap between their abilities and their goals. Research supports six major elements of scaffolding, ranging from preinstructional activities to applications to new examples.

Ann Brown and Joseph Campione argue that thinking must be incorporated in all school programs, even for the youngest children and those at risk. Their research-based programs illustrate "reciprocal teaching," which encourages thinking by organized cooperative discussions in reading, writing, and science.

Charles Letteri describes a means of assessing students' learning strengths and weaknesses. He shows how such diagnostic information can guide individualized and group programs of instruction to improve classroom performance.

Robert Ennis argues that one way to encourage thinking is to assess it, since students are guided by recognition and feedback. His goal is "reasonable reflective thinking focused on what to believe or do." He discusses several tests and techniques for measuring thinking for accountability.

Concluding Perspectives

Barry Beyer synthesizes current scholarship and practice under several components: a thoughtful learning environment, teaching thinking skills, direct instruction in skills teaching, teacher modeling, and integration of these components in all major subjects. He defines and illustrates each of these.

Robert Sternberg argues that thoughtful schools require thoughtful principals, teachers, and students. He shows how principals employ "the thinking cycle," consisting of problem recognition and definition, resource allocation, plan formulation, implementation, monitoring, and fine-tuning or revision.

James Keefe provides an analytic framework in the last chapter. It offers a continuum on which to classify and organize the approaches and serves as a conceptual matrix of what they contain.

Conclusion

Educators will find a wealth of ideas in these chapters. They have been chosen to represent a variety of philosophies and techniques. Given their personal viewpoints and settings, educators may indeed wish to seek a balance among these views. The matrix in James Keefe's chapter is a good starting place for pursuing this balance.

A final point about balance may serve to conclude this overview. Educators must strike a balance of knowledge and thought; they must seek other balances as well. Cognition itself must be balanced against emotion and behavior. As Plato declared, three horses pull the psychological chariot: feelings, thoughts, and behavior. Letting one element get too far ahead or headed in the wrong direction can upset the chariot—and skew the thinking curriculum.

References

Walberg, H. J. "Scientific Literacy and Economic Productivity in International Perspective." *Daedalus* 112(1983): 1–28.

———. "Synthesis of Research on Time and Learning." *Educational Leadership* 6(1988): 76–85.

CHAPTER 1

Thinking Skills in the Curriculum

Barbara Z. Presseisen

It is not surprising that a period of school reform includes a critical examination of the curriculum, as well as a review of practices in both instruction and assessment. Thus, the current movement to "restructure" American education is considering a variety of ways to organize what is learned at school, who makes such decisions, for what purposes and objectives, and under what kinds of conditions and constraints.

The last decade of the twentieth century is also marked by renewed interest in a social-cognitive approach to teaching and learning. Resting on a research base in human development and drawing on the explosion of knowledge in an information age, a focus on developing higher order thought processes has made the teaching of thinking throughout the school's curriculum a viable option for restructured schooling (Presseisen, 1987; Presseisen et al., 1990; Resnick and Klopfer, 1989). From all indications, this option is likely to persist and to influence classrooms in both critical and creative ways well into the 1990s.

What does such an approach mean to educators in the nation's secondary schools? What implications does it hold for the ways they organize student learning and assignments, for their conception of knowledge itself? Indeed, what might a thinking curriculum imply for both teachers and students in the academic as well as the work world of the 21st century?

Historical Perspective

For nearly 75 years, curriculum in American schools, and particularly its high schools, has largely been an accumulation of significant facts intricately woven into a tapestry of scholastic linguistics. "The knowledge of most worth" pursued in the nation's classrooms—even without a formalized national curriculum—has long involved a common vocabulary of academic labels: scope and sequence, subject-by-subject syllabi, course requirements, and discrete departmental subject matters usually defined by course textbooks or a state's general standards and regulations.

Under these circumstances, teaching has most often involved "telling" and "coverage," followed by a testing or assessment experience. In some ways, the curriculum of the most recent past in American education has been a "cultural heritage" amalgam.

In contrast, over the last decade, the movement to make the curriculum more thoughtful and the students more strategic problem solvers has passed through a series of changes that has gradually influenced particular subject matters in a fairly common way. Writing across the curriculum highlights the fact that active minds need to produce linguistic knowledge and not merely memorize it. The new guidelines in mathematics education stress problem solving and understanding the strategies of mathematical thought development. The rediscovery of the richness of literature reveals new forms of literacy for understanding how cultures connect writers and contexts. Science teaching is intrigued by the questions that scientists ask as well as by the formation of viable problems.

Subject-specific thinkers have been encouraged to focus on questioning protocols, and not merely on finding elusive answers to static situations that are guaranteed to change. A new-found aesthetic calls not only for appreciating the various graphic and plastic arts, but also for generating the discriminations and nuance-finding abilities required by critical evaluation. Finally, in a globally interdependent and technologically complex society, human understanding calls out for critical examination and culturally diverse ways of depicting reality that were once the province of a much simpler, and probably naive, "social studies."

In one sense, a whole new mindset has grown up around the nation's curricula. A different understanding about how students learn and acquire knowledge has gradually become accepted. Much of what transpires in educational practice can be understood more easily within the context of discovering what teaching for thinking means in the school's curriculum.

Comprehending the Thinking Curriculum

"Thinking skills" in the curriculum is probably a misnomer. An emphasis on acquiring discrete thinking skills could imply that thoughtfulness can be broken down into little bits of information which are merely aggregated to generate knowledge. In contrast, most of the current cognitive educational movement stresses building connections, having insights, and grasping intuitions that suggest knowledge is built in very different, nonreductionist ways.

Higher order thinking—the objective that drives many of the programs in this movement—includes processes or operations that are emergent over the long haul and require active, repeated interactions among the learner, the content, and the various learning experiences in school. Indeed, there are at least four distinctive aspects that we should examine in order to clarify teaching for thinking in the overall curriculum.

Central to the teaching of thinking is what is meant by *cognition* itself. Thinking is generally assumed to be a cognitive process or set of processes, mental acts by which long-term knowledge is acquired and remembered. Some scholars suggest that cognition actually is composed of multiple building blocks: perception, attention, learning, memory, reasoning, language, and emotion.

Much of the current educational movement concentrates on teaching reasoning ability to developing learners, especially the analytic qualities of critical thinking. There is also renewed interest in the development of memory and a concern with perceptual skills, spurred on by advances in video representation and computerized technology. At the same time, a fascination with the brain and its neural organization has opened additional elements of cognition and raised different research questions, such as Gardner's (Gardner and Hatch, 1989) queries into the dimensions of multiple intelligence. Potentially, cognition can introduce many exciting and innovative notions to curriculum development.

A second distinguishable aspect of thinking in the curriculum is a focus on *metacognition,* the learner's knowledge or awareness of his or her own cognitive processes and products and the ability to regulate them (feedback). In the current movement to place thinking at the heart of particular curricula, much has been emphasized that is metacognitive (executive skill-based).

In learning to think, the learner recognizes that he or she must deal with two kinds of knowledge: that which involves the learner as a doer of the thinking and the one ultimately responsible for it; and that which involves managing the processes of understanding a particular content, how it is organized, and what significance it has for resolving specific, real problems. Metacognition in the curriculum deals with both self-management and strategic, substantive operations.

A third distinguishable aspect of teaching for thinking in the curriculum concentrates on *conation,* the motivational striving or attempting to do something directly with a learning experience. The motivational or attitudinal aspects of behavior, including various dispositions, suggest that motivated thinkers may be inclined to develop and use practices. When learners are curious about their work, when tasks seem relevant to a personal context, or when problems translate to the real world of the student—even beyond the school or classroom—learning is more likely to occur. By contrast, research suggests that if such motivation is missing, even the best curriculum will probably fail.

And finally, the fourth aspect of teaching for thinking in the curriculum includes *epistemological* considerations—the nature of the subject content itself—how particular subject structures influence what is learned, the ways knowledge is characterized, the methods associated with defining and generating content, and the kinds of records or products with which students must be familiar to build a conceptual base.

Academic content has been the focus of curriculum development throughout the long history of schooling. What seems to be different about content at the end of the twentieth century is that the subject disciplines are viewed as developmental and in flux themselves. They have particular relationships to the other aspects of curricula (cognition, metacognition, conation) which must be considered when planning student programs and classroom instruction. In fact, the interaction among these four aspects of teaching for thinking in the curriculum is an appropriate focus for examining what is developing in curricular implementation in the schools.

New Programs and Their Implementation

At least two kinds of programs present thinking skills in emergent school curricula. First, there are those programs that teach thinking in a specialized format or theory, or for particular goals of thinking that they seek to develop. *Project Impact* aims to teach middle or high school students the skills of critical thinking and general problem solving. De Bono's *CoRT* program emphasizes the development of creative or lateral thinking abilities and seeks applications by youngsters as well as adults in life-in-general circumstances. In Lipman's *Philosophy for Children,* the content area (philosophy) is emphasized no more than the actual reasoning skills in student problem-solving activities.

A second type of thinking program is more typical of the school-developed curriculum, organized around particular subjects or courses, and generally rooted in textbooks and teacher manuals developed by national publishers. In this second type of program, teaching for thinking may be infused into the scope and sequence of a particular school course, or it may be integrated into the content of a basal or subject matter text.

It is this second type of program that is the subject of our discussion. Teachers are more likely to use these kinds of materials in their instruction at school. These programs usually figure in school-based decision making about curriculum. Our emphasis does not negate the use of the first kind of thinking program. Valid reasons exist for educators to consider employing these specialized thinking materials. Research studies are available that discuss their successful use (Chance, 1986).

For an initial experience, however, materials from the second type of program are more likely to be incorporated into teacher training in teaching for thinking. It is also possible to examine implementation of the four aspects of teaching for thinking in the curriculum in terms of these materials.

Cognition and the Curriculum

By far, the most common cognitive emphasis on teaching for thinking in the curriculum involves determining what are the essential (basic) and higher order skills or processes, developing common definitions or meanings for these several abilities, and helping teachers see that these operations are actually embedded in good teaching and sound curricula.

Marzano et al. (1988), Beyer (1988), and Swartz and Perkins (1989) are well-known studies that have stressed this approach. Closely related are added emphases on memory, not merely for purposes of memorization, but rather to make information more manageable for the learner. Students are encouraged to master memory techniques by enhancing verbal or visual cues, by increasing voluntary attention and awareness, and by being more cognizant of perceptual limitations and constraints in their studies.

Looking at both elementary and secondary textbooks, one can easily find examples of various thinking abilities translated into lessons for learning science, history, language arts, and mathematics in the classroom. These sources relate thinking abilities to specific subject content. Examples of such lessons in current classroom materials include:

- Comparing an amoeba and a macrophage in biology for similarities and differences (a secondary program).

- Predicting the consequences of poor garbage control in a heavily populated neighborhood (an elementary program).

- Analyzing a chart from the *World Almanac* listing animal running speeds—finding what are "typical" and comparing them to human ability and performance (a middle school task).

- Following sequential information in a story and being able to summarize it in a comprehensive way (elementary and secondary programs, depending on the complexity of the literature used).

The various aspects of cognition raise questions about how a curriculum is organized and presented. One researcher interested in memory influences on student learning suggests that education should extend the period of time during which students acquire specific (mathematical) knowledge. He asks whether the traditional course-per-year in middle/high school mathematics (general mathematics, followed by introductory algebra, geometry, and advanced algebra) may actually negatively influence the amount and quality of mathematics retained by students over time.

Questions may need to be raised about students' familiarity with particular knowledge, as well as the appropriateness of tasks assigned in actual course instruction. Cognition in the curriculum gets at the heart of what is to be learned. At the same time, it raises issues about how such information is acquired and what a student's task experience should be for the most effective retention.

Metacognition and the Curriculum

A focus on metacognition in the classroom emphasizes helping students understand their own responses to thoughtful situations. Quite often, metacognition or executive control involves "hands-on" learning strategies to help the learner represent the information more vividly and to suggest routes to solutions embedded in particular contents. It presumes that direct contact and visual representation can depict larger, perhaps more subtle, issues. In the thinking classroom, tacit understandings of a problem situation should be discussed, group interaction encouraged, and learners made aware of the characteristics of the information under scrutiny. Metacognition seeks to make student learning more explicit and the products of classroom experiences more memorable.

A thinking curriculum that includes metacognitive skills often emphasizes planning, monitoring, and evaluating behaviors that can gradually be taught to students as the particular content is examined. Consider these problem-solving strategies, seen from a teacher's perspective, as applied to the learning of science *before, during,* and *after* a particular classroom experiment.

- *Before the task*

    1. Discuss the nature of the problem being studied.

    2. Ask students questions to help them understand the problem.

    3. Discuss the prior knowledge that students might apply.

    4. Discuss possible solution strategies.

- *During the task*

    5. Observe and question students.

    6. Give information or limited hints, as needed.

    7. Be sure that students check their answers, strategies.

8. Have an extension problem ready for early finishers or a more difficult task for more able performers.

■ *After the task*

9. Discuss the various solutions. Ask students to name and describe the strategies they used.

10. Discuss the extension problems or different tasks. Compare the various problems/tasks.

11. Discuss errors students have made and why they occurred.

12. Discuss possible pitfalls of similar problems and what can be done about them.

13. Have students write similar problems with new material, different media, or slightly different content. Compare these and have students discuss what happens in these variations.

14. Have students write test questions employing similar problems; try them. Compare the strategies used and the solutions obtained. Have students keep logs or journals about their observations.

15. Have student groups design related, more complex problems.

The important role of the teacher as questioner—prodder and elaborator—emerges from understanding the significance of metacognition in the thinking curriculum. How can an instructor encourage students to clarify their ideas, to analyze more deeply, to raise significant, even risky, new concepts? How can the teacher stress accuracy and strategic power in the learning tasks developed?

The teacher as trusted mediator is a key metacognitive role; the role of assessor is diminished. Teaching materials are needed to support constructive interaction and the teacher's new mediational role in the classroom. The merging of curricular and instructional tasks is part of this approach.

The thinking classroom that emphasizes metacognition is bent on heightened awareness (Prawat, 1989). The larger goal involves accessing

learning strategies and being able to know and transfer successful practices to similar but different problems. Teaching for thinking metacogni-
tively means helping students learn how to learn, as much as developing
the cognitive operations themselves.

Student success at school is directly related to "what the students do
with the information presented . . . what sense they make of it, how they
relate to what they know and believe" (Wittrock, 1987).

In contrast to traditional curricula, which focus on static, accumulated
knowledge, the newer published programs emphasize *dynamic* use and
active involvement of both students and teachers in the learning task.

Motivation and the Curriculum

Whereas cognition and metacognition strive to make the learner more
skillful, motivation views the developing learner as willful and purposeful. The "student as worker" metaphor employed in the new curricula of
the Coalition of Essential Schools mirrors this view. This conception car-
ries with it implications for a curriculum that is "authentic." Problems
must ring true to the students, such as a citizenship unit concerned with
how a person knows when he or she is "good."

An authentic curriculum implies learning relationships that are active
and, more important, self-regulative. It accepts the premise that interesting instruction and well-constructed learning tasks will evoke questions
from students, tap natural curiosity, and spark personal energy for future
inquiry. Such a curriculum is designed as an intellectual challenge; the
problem tasks are forged in a student's long-term involvement with
essential content, and a gradual building of integrated knowledge.

Motivation is very much involved with attitudes about learning and
thinking that are developed over rather long periods of time. How does
the learner cope with error or failure? How does a teacher guide students
when they are selecting a weak strategy? Even more significant, is the
student developing a self-concept as a knower of knowledge and a keeper
of the standards that such academic pursuit entails? The thinking curriculum calls for the student to direct his or her own thinking as content
is encountered.

Motivation raises issues of what it means to become a scientist, a historian, or a writer, and how one performs responsibly along the road from novice to expert. It may mean that students need to see an event from several points of view and only slowly learn to value one perspective as more valid. It may mean that eager workers must learn to curb their impulsivity, to hold back judgment until additional information is available. It may mean that only in retrospect does the learner appreciate a teacher's emphasis on greater deliberation and further information gathering.

The role of teacher as mediator is a key to useful motivation. And the curriculum can play an important part by providing learning tasks that are intellectually challenging and provocative to curious students. Equally important in such a curriculum are problems that encourage the student to reflect or to talk with their peers as they actually work through assignments or homework. Socially demanding or cooperative tasks are now frequently found in new curricular materials.

The student who is an *autonomous* learner is the prime mover of the knowledge base. Seeking better information becomes natural to the student. Access to resources, the free exchange of findings, and uncovering and exploring belief systems are part of learning any content. In addition, the classroom environment, within which a thinking curriculum is explored, is motivational as well as supportive of cognition and metacognition. Intellectual pursuits are treasured. Respect for differing opinions is not merely tolerated, but is encouraged.

Singular answers or all-encompassing solutions may be rare. It is their pursuit that must be taken seriously by both students and teachers. And classroom materials must meet these criteria. Indeed, promoting motivation in the thinking curriculum is a subtle challenge.

Subject Content and the Curriculum

What are the subjects we study at school? Is the curriculum merely the sum of its parts or is it something more significant? Teaching content in the thinking curriculum is concerned with disciplinary, even interdisciplinary, development and change. This aspect of teaching for thinking is also mindful that formal knowledge is a socially constructed product.

The curricular challenge today is no different than what Socrates faced centuries ago: How to bring the findings of mature scholars to the minds of young learners and at the same time, to present the materials so that students, although limited in their mastery, can be active in their exploration?

Transfer is a basic concern of learning in any content area. How can the learner apply successful strategies to more than one subject matter? What is required to make such a match? How can students use the prior knowledge they possess in new or novel ways? How can educators develop more integrative curricula, reducing the fragmentation in student programs?

Recent projects in science (Project 2061), and guidelines for implementation of the new secondary mathematics, are beginning to address these substantive issues in the curriculum. Other content areas, such as the various social sciences, still need to identify a more holistic theme in order to build unity in their particular, underlying disciplines.

Perhaps some notions about higher order thinking can help these deliberations. Consider, for example, the parallel conceptual underpinnings of history, anthropology, and psychology. How do the processes of cognition and metacognitive awareness relate to these basic conceptual understandings?

Teaching for thinking, so far as it has developed as a new strategy of curriculum/instructional reform, has yet to answer even some of the most basic epistemological questions. It has uncovered some very interesting issues that have been relatively untouched since the last spate of curriculum reform.

A great deal still must be done in research and practice. It would seem that fostering research about these subtle relationships should be an important aspect of teacher education as well as of materials development. Such understandings about content are also likely to affect the new curricula, classroom instruction, and student assessment.

Implications for Education and Educators

Teaching for thinking in the curriculum involves at least four major concerns for educators:

1. Thinking skills are not mere add-ons to a curriculum already packed

with information and facts. Teaching for thinking is a social-cognitive enterprise that must focus on how students learn and acquire knowledge across the broad sequence of academic courses.

2. Thinking in a curriculum is a dynamic process that requires students to reflect and share with their colleagues in interactive ways. Learning to think is a social phenomenon that may begin with concrete, hands-on learning tasks but gradually should become more self-directed and conceptual.

3. Learning to think about a particular curriculum involves a personal commitment to scholarly work and to strategies of direct engagement. A student acquiring new thinking skills must have the motivation to be involved and to make successful acts his or her usual performance.

4. Thinking in a content area requires a holistic, conceptual understanding of that area and the rules or standards that shape it. Thinking generally lies beyond the artificial divisions of curriculum that have characterized school programs in the past. A thinking curriculum should make it easier for students to work flexibly across their several subject matters.

These concerns have not been resolved by American education; rather, they have only been realized. Curriculum developers have begun an enthusiastic integration of higher order skills into content areas, but much remains to be done beyond that.

All four aspects of teaching for thinking need attention in educational practice. In the final analysis, however, these understandings may provide a new meaning for curriculum itself. Instead of the repository-of-cultural-heritage approach so long the *raison d être* of schooling, curriculum today promises to become a major tool of learning. Curriculum can and should enable teachers to invent or transform meanings *with* students, to confront realities of the world, and to turn them into mindful understandings.

In the words of Piaget, to know something is to invent it. A curriculum for thinking is a heady invention.

References

Beyer, B. K. *Developing a Thinking Skills Program.* Boston: Allyn and Bacon, 1988.

Chance, P. *Thinking in the Classroom: A Survey of Programs.* New York: Teachers College, Columbia University, 1986.

Gardner, H., and Hatch, T. "Multiple Intelligences Go to School." *Educational Researcher,* November 1989.

Marzano, R. J.; Brandt, R. S.; Hughes, C. S.; Jones B. F.; Presseisen, B. Z.; Rankin, S. C.; and Suhor, C. *Dimensions of Thinking: A Framework for Curriculum and Instruction.* Alexandria, Va.: Association for Supervision and Curriculum Development, 1988.

Prawat, R. S. "Promoting Access to Knowledge, Strategy, and Disposition in Students: A Research Synthesis." *Review of Educational Research,* Spring 1989.

Presseisen, B. Z. *Thinking Skills Throughout the Curriculum: A Conceptual Design.* Bloomington, Ind.: Pi Lambda Theta, 1987.

Presseisen, B. Z.; Sternberg, R. J.; Fischer, K. W.; Knight, C.; and Feuerstein, R. *Learning and Thinking Styles: Classroom Interaction.* Washington, D.C., and Philadelphia, Pa.: National Education Association and Research for Better Schools, 1990.

Resnick, L. B., and Klopfer, L. E., eds. *Toward the Thinking Curriculum: Current Cognitive Research.* Alexandria, Va.: Association for Supervision and Curriculum Development, 1989.

Swartz, R. J., and Perkins, D. N. *Teaching Thinking: Issues and Approaches.* Pacific Grove, Calif.: Midwest Publications, 1989.

Wittrock, M. C. "Teaching and Student Thinking." *Journal of Teacher Education,* November–December 1987.

CHAPTER 2

A Rationale and Framework for Teaching Thinking Tactics

Robert J. Marzano

The notion of teaching tactics for thinking is relatively new, at least as a regular classroom practice. Fundamentally, teaching thinking tactics involves teaching strategies for performing mental or physical operations where a strategy can be understood as a general set of rules or steps that will help you perform a task. Usually there is no strict sequence to the steps used within a strategy, although there is a general flow of activity.

For example, a general strategy exists for reading a book that includes such components as looking at the cover, scanning the table of contents, scanning the pictures, and so on. Although no one step necessarily must be performed before (or after) another, there is a general flow of activity.

Teaching thinking tactics, then, involves presenting students with general steps to be taken when performing specific cognitive operations. The notion is gaining considerable momentum because of the strength of the research findings supporting it. Specifically, teaching explicit tactics for specific types of thinking has been shown to dramatically change student performance in such areas as reading comprehension, decision making, problem solving, writing, and a host of other types of tasks. (For a summary of the research on strategy instructions see Derry and Murphy, 1986, in the list of suggested readings.)

The fact that strategy instruction works is no longer in question. Neither is there any question about who should be taught thinking strategies.

Who Should Be Taught

The fact is indisputable that those who most need instruction in thinking tactics receive the least amount of it. Specifically, strategy instruction is most important for at-risk students; yet, as a group, they commonly do not receive such instruction. Conversely, many of the thinking tactics that are necessary to process information and deeply understand it are already known by middle and high achievers. They commonly learn these strategies in the rich information processing background from which they come.

Students from all socioeconomic strata engage in far too many passive cognitive activities such as watching television, but students from middle and high-income families:

- Are read to more in their homes

- Have more in-depth discussions on substantive topics in their home

- Live in a much more complex informational environment.

It is this complex environment that allows more privileged youngsters to spontaneously develop strategies for learning and thinking. Additionally, their parents engage in more implicit mediated instruction. Mediated instruction means gradually guiding a learner in the understanding and eventual mastery of the steps in a complex strategy.

At first, the adult offers a great deal of guidance to the learner, including an overt model of the strategy. The adult gradually decreases the amount of guidance (except when needed) to allow the learner to shape the strategy and adapt it to his or her own needs and style.

To understand how mediated instruction is commonly practiced in some homes, consider the example of a parent helping a child with a homework assignment in mathematics. The parent might first talk the child through a few of the problems, suggesting some key steps necessary to solving such problems. Next, the parent might ask the child to try solving some problems using the steps that were modeled.

As the child tries the steps, the parent offers suggestions, providing gentle guidance as needed. Eventually, the parent completely withdraws his or her help when it is apparent that the child can perform the homework task independently.

Even when mediated instruction is not done properly, the parent usually provides an explicit model for the strategies needed to complete the homework task. This informal, yet powerful, instruction allows many students to acquire the thinking tactics necessary for academic success.

Unfortunately, not all children come from home environments where such mediated instruction occurs. In fact, the recent national "report cards" on mathematics, reading, and writing from the National Assessment of Educational Progress indicated that this type of home instruction is lacking for at-risk students, most of whom come from minority and low socioeconomic status groups.

This fact alone validates the need for the direct teaching of thinking. There is some disagreement, however, about how this should occur.

How Thinking Should be Taught

There is a continuum of the ways to teach thinking strategies. At one end are approaches that teach thinking explicitly in a content-free environment. At the other end are approaches that embed skills within the teaching of content. The former is commonly referred to as the explicit approach. The latter is called the implicit approach.

Barry Beyer is probably the most widely recognized proponent of the explicit approach. Beyer asserts that there are five steps to teaching a thinking strategy. First, the teacher introduces the strategy. This includes describing and demonstrating the steps, explaining when the strategy should be used, and naming the strategy. If a teacher were introducing a summarizing strategy, he or she would first demonstrate it to students by illustrating each of the steps, then explain that they can use the strategy whenever they need to capture a large amount of information in an abridged fashion, and finally tell them that the name of the technique is "summarizing."

During the second step, students would experiment with the strategy in a content-neutral manner. The teacher would provide students with familiar and interesting contents, allowing them to focus on the summarizing strategy without the interference of new or uninteresting content.

The third step of Beyer's model has students reflecting on what goes on in their minds as they use the summarizing strategy and articulating their insights. This might be done in cooperative groups.

As a result of the discussion, during the fourth step, students would make changes in the strategy. Students might determine, for example, that they have to add a step or two to those initially modeled by the teacher.

Finally, in the fifth step, students would try out the modified strategy and again reflect on its use.

Beyer believes that, in general, students need the extensive and direct instruction provided by his model before they can use a thinking strategy independently.

Perhaps the most widely used program with an explicit, content-free approach is Edward de Bono's CoRT program. The program acquired its name from de Bono's organization, the Cognitive Research Trust. CoRT contains some 60 thinking strategies organized into six levels. Each strategy is taught in a content-free environment, and is practiced by students until they can use it independently.

At the other end of the continuum are approaches to thinking that attempt to teach it implicitly. Steps to thinking strategies are not overtly taught, but are embedded in content instruction.

Lauren Resnick is perhaps the most visible proponent of the implicit approach. She asserts that thinking does not occur in isolation; we utilize various cognitive strategies only in so far as they help us learn and use content. She suggests that the tasks students are asked to perform while learning content should model specific types of thinking.

In a social studies class, for example, when asking students to investigate why President Truman ordered the use of the atomic bomb during World War II, a teacher must also reinforce the thinking strategies involved in the mental process of investigation. Similarly, while requiring students to develop a new way of classifying elements in a science class, the teacher should reinforce the mental process of classification.

Figure 1. Tactics for Thinking

Learning-To-Learn Strategies

- Attention Control—Strengthens concentration and lengthens attention span
- Deep Processing—Raises memory potential and depth of information processing
- Memory Frameworks—Helps students recall key information

- Power Thinking—Cultivates better student attitudes toward their own capabilities
- Goal Setting—Helps students create a vision for their own success
- The Responsibility Frame—Boosts students' ability to learn independently

Content Thinking Strategies

- Concept Attainment—Introduces a method for understanding new concepts
- Concept Development—Provides a way to study new concepts in depth
- Pattern Recognition—Improves ability to organize and comprehend spoken or written information
- Macro-Pattern Recognition—Expands comprehension of large bodies of information
- Synthesizing—Teaches a method for integrating large amounts of new knowledge
- Proceduralizing—Shows students how to learn new skills

Reasoning Strategies

- Analogical Reasoning—Prepares students for aptitude tests and helps them see relationships
- Extrapolation—Helps students see relationships between information at an abstract level
- Evaluation of Evidence—Develops ability to analyze information for accuracy and relevance
- Examination of Value—Shows how to objectively analyze differing views on a controversial topic
- Non-Linguistic Patterns—Identifies numeric, spatial, and recursive patterns
- Elaboration—Demonstrates how to infer from reading
- Solving Everyday Problems—Provides a framework for analytical problem solving
- Solving Academic Problems—Equips students with tactics for solving school-related problems
- Invention—Stimulates creative thinking and development of unique but meaningful products.

No program is directly designed to implement the implicit approach, but Richard Paul's techniques come very close. Paul's program specifies for teachers how to redesign lessons to implicitly reinforce a variety of critical thinking strategies.

In addition to the programs at the two ends of the thinking skills instructional continuum, a variety of programs exist at various points between the extremes. Administrators and teachers have available a variety of options to teach and reinforce thinking. (For a review of the various programs, see the compendiums by Chance and Costa.)

In the remainder of this chapter, a program is described that attempts to combine elements from the explicit and implicit ends of the continuum.

Tactics for Thinking: A Compromise Approach

Tactics for Thinking is a program that includes strategies for increasing competency in 22 cognitive skills (see Figure 1). The 22 strategies within the program are organized into three broad categories: learning-to-learn strategies, content thinking strategies, and reasoning strategies.

Learning To Learn

The tactics within the learning-to-learn section of the program provide student strategies for regulating their own information processing and learning in ways that are personally meaningful and easily accessible. For example, the tactic of Attention Control makes students aware of their responsibility to pay attention (even in situations in which they do not find it easy) and suggests specific techniques for doing so.

Similarly, the tactic of Power Thinking alerts students to the need to monitor and control their attitudes about completing specific classroom tasks and provides techniques for doing so. The tactics of Deep Processing and Memory Frameworks help students use various aspects of imagery (e.g., mental pictures, physical sensations, and emotions) to integrate information into their existing knowledge base in such a way that it is easily retrieved and used.

Content Thinking

The content thinking tactics are designed to help students comprehend and more deeply process information presented by the teacher or the textbook. Tactics in this category deal with both declarative and procedural information.

Declarative information ("what") is a knowledge of concepts, principles, and various types of schema within a given content area. The tactics of Concept Attainment and Concept Development help students initially acquire and then ultimately make fine distinctions about important concepts. The Pattern Recognition tactic helps students organize and process principles and information that conform to such organizational schemata as time sequences and causal networks.

Procedural information is more process oriented ("how to"). The tactic of Proceduralizing is intended to help students identify and articulate the important steps in content-related processes. It helps students set up a practice schedule to use the process under study until they have mastered it.

Reasoning

The reasoning tactics are designed to help students use information in ways that expand and restructure their understanding of content. The Extrapolation tactic, for example, helps students understand how the abstractions underlying one piece of information also support another piece of information. The Evaluation of Evidence tactic helps students analyze information for its validity and relevancy. The Invention tactic helps students use information to create unique but meaningful products.

Implementation

The tactics program provides students with explicit instruction in thinking strategies, but it is not meant to be used as a "pull-out" program. The strategies are not designed to be taught in a separate course, isolated from content. Rather, they should be used in a regular classroom situation to enhance students' learning of important content.

At first, the strategies must be cued by the teacher. For example, a teacher might begin a class by reminding students of the Attention Control tactic and guiding them through its use to increase their instructional focus. Then the teacher might present a new concept using the Concept

Attainment or Concept Development tactics. Finally, he or she might help students see how the new concept relates to other concepts through the Extrapolation tactic.

When students have internalized the tactics, they then can use them without aid or cuing from the teacher. A student might notice that she is not focused on the lesson and use the Attention Control tactic to enhance her readiness for learning. As the teacher presents the lesson, the student might decide to use aspects of the Concept Development tactic to help her understand an important concept that has been presented. Finally, she might decide to use aspects of the Extrapolation tactic to make connections, not explicit in the lesson, with other information she has learned.

Ultimately, the Tactics program is a way for teachers, schools, or districts to begin exploring the teaching of thinking. It is not meant to be implemented as a complete program, but teachers, schools, or districts can select those tactics that they find most useful for particular content areas or classrooms.

Teachers are also encouraged to adapt the strategies to meet their specific needs. Many of those who use the program, for example, collapse aspects of the Concept Attainment tactic and the Concept Development tactic into a single strategy that guides students through the initial introduction of a concept to its mature development. At a more formal level, some schools and districts embed selected tactics into their curriculum objectives. They select specific tactics from the list of 22 to be taught at specific grade levels or in specific content areas. Figure 2 shows eight tactics selected by a given school: Attention Control, Deep Processing, Power Thinking, Concept Attainment, Pattern Recognition, Extrapolation, Evaluation of Evidence, and Everyday Problem Solving.

The school has determined that Attention Control will be taught at the second grade level as an aspect of classroom rules and procedures. Deep Processing will be taught at the third grade level as part of language arts, and so on. In this way, various tactics are systematically introduced into the curriculum without burdening teachers or students.

Individual tactics can also be taught prior to their designated introduction. A third grade teacher, for example, might decide to introduce Pattern Recognition as part of her reading class, even though that tactic was not slated to be generally introduced until the fourth grade. Specifying where selected tactics should be taught in the curriculum simply ensures that students will be introduced to them sometime in their school experience.

Figure 2. Sample Placement of Selected Tactics in Curriculum

Tactic Introduced	Grade Level/Content Area
Attention Control	Second grade: classroom rules and procedures
Deep Processing	Third grade: language arts
Power Thinking	Third grade: classroom rules and procedures
Concept Attainment	Third grade: science
Pattern Recognition	Fourth grade: reading
Extrapolation	Fifth grade: social studies
Evaluation of Evidence	Sixth grade: social studies
Everyday Problem Solving	Seventh grade: health

Thus, teachers can know which tactics students have been exposed to and not waste valuable class time introducing those tactics. Knowing that Extrapolation has been taught at the fifth grade level as part of social studies instruction allows the sixth grade science teacher to use it without having to teach it. Of course, some review and reteaching may be necessary.

Since its inception, the Tactics program has been extensively tested and has been shown to enhance students' performance in the strategies that are taught as well as improve their performance on standardized tests. (For a summary of the evaluations of the program, see Marzano, 1989.) *Tactics for Thinking* (Marzano and Arredondo, 1986) is a good place to start. It is simply a set of cognitive strategies to be taught by teachers and used by students to enhance control over and facility with the learning process. Once a few selected tactics have been introduced by the teacher and internalized by students, both can move on to more complex, and more self-initiated, learning strategies.

In the final analysis, the teaching of thinking will not be accomplished by adopting a program or a set of practices. Rather, it requires a commitment on the part of administrators, teachers, and parents to rethink their educational goals in curriculum, instruction, and assessment and to plan school improvement initiatives that incorporate thinking strategies.

Suggested Readings

Beyer, B. K. *Developing a Thinking Skills Program.* Boston, Mass.: Allyn & Bacon, 1988.

Chance, P. *Thinking in the Classroom.* New York: Teacher's College Press, 1986.

Costa, A., ed. *Developing Minds: A Resource Book for the Teaching of Thinking.* Alexandria, Va.: Association for Supervision and Curriculum Development, 1985.

de Bono, E. "The CoRT Thinking Program." In *Thinking and Learning Skills: Vol. 1. Relating Instruction to Research,* edited by J. W. Segal, S. F. Chipman, and R. Glaser. Hillsdale, N.J.: Erlbaum, 1985.

Derry, S. J., and Murphy, D. A. "Designing Systems That Train Learning Ability: From Theory into Practice." *Review of Educational Research* 1(1986): 1–39.

Marzano, R. J. *A Summary Report: Evaluation of the Tactics for Thinking Program.* Aurora, Colo.: Mid-continent Regional Educational Laboratory, 1989. (ERIC Document Reproduction Service No. ED 314 710.)

Marzano, R. J., and Arredondo, D. E. *Tactics for Thinking.* Alexandria, Va.: Association for Supervision and Curriculum Development, 1986.

Marzano, R. J.; Brandt, R. S.; Hughes, C. S.; Jones, B. F.; Presseisen, B. Z.; Rankin, S. C.; and Suhor, C. *Dimensions of Thinking: A Framework for Curriculum and Instruction.* Alexandria, Va.: Association for Supervision and Curriculum Development, 1988.

Paul, R.; Binker, A. S. A.; and Charbonneau, M. *Critical Thinking Handbooks: K-3, A Guide for Remodeling Lesson Plans in Language, Arts, Social Studies, and Science.* Rohnert Park, Calif.: Sonoma State University, Center for Critical Thinking and Moral Critique, 1986.

Resnick, L. B. *Education and Learning To Think.* Washington, D.C.: National Academy Press, 1987.

CHAPTER 3

Nurturing Thoughtfulness

Francis Schrag

Teaching students *how* to think rather than *what* to think is not a new idea, but it is one that has caught fire among educators and educational writers during the past decade. Unfortunately, there has not been enough thinking about what it means to teach people how to think.

How To Think About Thinking

To many educators, teaching students how to think is like teaching any set of skills, such as driving a car, adding fractions, or writing a business letter. The teacher's job is to break down a complex activity into its component parts, to demonstrate and explain how to perform each component, to provide plenty of opportunity for practice, and then to supply feedback. I don't think this is a fruitful way to think about teaching thinking.

As I see it, teaching students to be better thinkers is more like teaching them to be courageous than like teaching them to drive a car. Let me explain this perhaps puzzling statement.

My favorite analogy for thinking about thinking is territorial exploration: Thinking is the mental counterpart of exploration. Just as explorers need different skills and different information depending on the terrain, so thinkers need different skills and different information depending on the domain they are working in. One cannot be an effective thinker without the relevant skills and information. Yet, the possession of skills and information does not by itself guarantee success in solving problems any more than in exploration. The explorer needs courage, determination, and sound judgment regardless of terrain. I call these character traits or, to use an apt if old-fashioned term, virtues. Likewise, the effective thinker, regardless of domain, needs to be thought-full.[1]

Just as courage does not lie so much in mastering a difficult skill as in resisting temptation to flee from or concede to powerful forces, so thoughtfulness involves being able to resist the temptation to act impulsively or in a stereotyped manner. The good thinker avoids precipitous action and avoids getting stuck in a rigid response. He or she is deliberate as well as flexible.

What are the advantages of my way of thinking about thinking? There are several: First, it makes it less likely that we will fool ourselves into believing that equipping students with any set of skills, procedures, recipes, or formulas is teaching them to be better thinkers. Second, my formulation prevents us from supposing that we can set aside one part of the day or the week to teach thinking as an additional subject on a par with arithmetic, driver's education, and the like. Third, my formulation prohibits our focusing our efforts on just one part of the school population or one curriculum area. Finally, it forces us to focus our attention on some of the conditions in and out of the school that weaken our efforts to promote better thinking. This last point requires elaboration.

Suppose we wanted to teach young people to be courageous. We would need to exhibit courage ourselves; and we would need to immerse students in environments in which courage was both needed and held in high esteem. The same goes for thoughtfulness. If we wish to cultivate thoughtfulness in the young, we must model it ourselves, and we must design environments that both elicit and reward it.

Are Schools Places for Thinking?

Is the conventional classroom well-designed to elicit and reward thoughtfulness? To answer this, consider a spectrum of settings that support thoughtfulness to different degrees. On one end of the spectrum are those settings that are least supportive of thoughtfulness. The factory assembly line, where each worker is expected to perform a single task every so many seconds or minutes, is the best example.

Now consider an environment at the other end of the spectrum—the scientific laboratory. The structure of the laboratory includes a number of features that reinforce thoughtfulness:

---

1. I am not using "thoughtful" here to mean "showing regard for others," although I believe there is a connection between the two meanings.

■ A high degree of autonomy accorded the problem solver, especially so far as the allocation of time is concerned.

■ Extensive collaboration among members of the laboratory requires them to move about freely. (This collaboration within the group is complemented, of course, by fierce competition between groups.)

■ Norms and procedures exist which ensure that the results and those responsible for them are publicized beyond the laboratory.

■ Norms and procedures are in place that reward both the originality of a contribution and its defensibility.

Note that these features of laboratory science are not present primarily to make scientists feel good about their work, but rather to facilitate the scientific work itself. These characteristics are present to some degree in all environments that require thoughtfulness, from medical clinics to automobile service stations.

Schools are not assembly lines, but the similarity between factories and schools has been noted, not just by wild-eyed opponents of traditional education but by responsible critics and observers such as Albert Shanker, president of the American Federation of Teachers. The fact is that schools rarely provide students with the kinds of tasks that require thoughtfulness; i.e., tasks that are challenging, long term, open ended, difficult to assess in a mechanical way, and that invite collaboration among students. The absence of such tasks and the conventional classroom setting make it possible for schools to divide the day into 45-minute periods, to provide uniform, frequent, and easily assessed examinations, and to discourage collaboration.

I do not believe that the typical classroom in the typical school is this way because of either ignorance or ill-will on the part of teachers and principals. Indeed, I argued in *Thinking in School and Society* (1988, p. 101) that the factory-like environment of most schools is an "intelligent adaptation of rational actors to perceived imperatives." What leads to the factory model, on my analysis, is two "givens" of schooling: the compulsoriness of schooling together with a grading system in which some can "win" only if others "lose."

These givens create a continual threat of disorder on the part of those who must continue to attend school, even if they do not perceive their chances of winning to be very high. It is teachers' perceptions of this threat that makes it rational for them to assign tasks that resemble those of the assembly line more than those of the laboratory.

Must we accept these givens? Our commitment to universal high school completion is not likely to waver, even though it is still far from a reality. Although experiments with alternative grading systems have been tried over the years, conventional systems will remain dominant so long as school grades are used as criteria for entrance to selective colleges.

There are exceptions to this factory pattern, to be sure, but careful study of such examples reveals that they are likely to be found either in classes where students are unusually motivated (or few in number), or where teachers exhibit unusual talent. We cannot expect to make these exceptional classrooms the general rule.

This does not mean that we must throw up our hands in despair, but neither should we deceive ourselves about the dimensions of the challenge. There are, I believe, two directions we can explore:

■ We can create more "thoughtful" settings that supplement the conventional classroom.

■ We can raise the level of thoughtfulness in the conventional classroom incrementally.

Creating New Settings for Thinking

The challenge of creating new settings that reward thoughtfulness requires imagination, experimentation, and a willingness to take risks. Fortunately, we are not without models both within and outside the school. If we look within a high school, the school newspaper provides us with a setting that demands thoughtfulness; indeed, here is a setting that embodies many of the features of its real-world counterpart. The editors and reporters collaborate; the authors are publicly identified and accountable for their stories; the work cannot be confined to a particular place or time, and so on.

I believe that we must invent new settings which, like the school newspaper, demand and reward thoughtfulness. One idea I have proposed is the social policy research institute, or "junior think tank" as I like to call it. A group of interested students under adult guidance from either a teacher or a professional policy analyst, would focus on a problem of concern to the adolescent and adult community: teenage pregnancy, drugs, racial hostility, or the dropout problem, to name a few possibilities. The group would meet once or twice a week, either in or out of school, and for several hours at a time. As in adult policy centers, the goal would be to learn as much about the problem as possible and to make recommendations to the school and community administrations.

The group would develop its own agenda as it went along, with only the general mission agreed upon at the outset. Students would encounter and need to resolve questions dealing with a range of issues from the ethic of confidentiality, to problems of research design, to the most effective way to present their results. Pilot projects might try out different ways of dealing with some of these problems. Consultants could be called on as the need arose.

Although the adult leader would supervise the effort, the adolescents would be allowed to make their own mistakes. Students would be introduced to some techniques and concepts needed to carry out the work, and would look at examples produced by adult centers, but there would be no expectation that the group would employ the sophisticated techniques available to adult policy researchers. Whatever skills or ideas had to be mastered would be learned only because of the actual requirements of the project. The project would be expected to issue a report to the entire community.

If school leaders are serious about teaching thinking, they must not only experiment with new ideas like the junior think tank, but also change their thinking about some of the activities that, like the newspaper, already exist but are considered peripheral to the educational program.

Many high schools host a wide range of activities such as science fairs, peer courts and counseling programs, filmmaking, and debating clubs, which demand thinking of the highest order. These programs often elicit a level of student and faculty commitment that is not found in the classroom. I daresay that many of these activities have more educational merit than those that take place within the curriculum.

I favor importing them into the regular school week and making them part of the curriculum. If a wide range of such activities were available, every student could be a participant in an activity of his or her choice. If more students want to write for a newspaper than the editors and faculty adviser can find room for, the principal should find an additional faculty member interested in guiding the publication of a rival newspaper.

All this is easier to propose than to carry out, and I must admit that the suggestions made so far require a degree of restructuring that may be unrealistic for many schools, but the perspective argued for in this chapter applies to the conventional classroom setting as well.

Promoting Thoughtfulness in the Classroom

Can we identify the characteristics of classrooms that foster thoughtfulness? Building upon my conception of good thinking, a group of researchers at the National Center on Effective Secondary Schools (NCESS), under the leadership of Fred Newmann, has been occupied with this question for several years.[2] The research has so far focused exclusively on social studies, but the criteria for "thoughtful lessons" we have evolved would appear to apply to a wide range of subject matters.

Our team developed a set of rating scales for "thoughtful lessons" which was ultimately reduced to six main dimensions. Teachers and administrators concerned about improving the quality of thinking in their schools might adopt or adapt these scales to assess thoughtfulness in their classrooms.

Dimension 1. There was sustained examination of a few topics rather than superficial coverage of many.

Thoughtfulness is supported by in-depth study and sustained concentration on a limited number of topics or questions. Lessons that cover a large number of topics give students only a vague familiarity or awareness and, thereby, reduce the possibilities for building the complex knowledge and

---

2. A comprehensive summary of the methods and results of this research project may be found in Newmann's chapter, listed at the end of this chapter.

skills required to understand a topic.

Dimension 2. The lesson displayed substantive coherence and continuity.

Progress toward understanding complex topics demands systematic inquiry that builds on relevant, accurate, and substantive knowledge in the field, and that works toward the logical development and integration of ideas. In contrast, lessons that teach material as unrelated fragments of knowledge, without pulling them together, undermine such inquiry.

Dimension 3. Students were given an appropriate amount of time to think; that is, to prepare responses to questions.

Thinking takes time, but often recitation, discussion, and written assignments pressure students to make responses before they have had enough time to reflect. Promoting thoughtfulness, therefore, requires periods of silence where students can ponder the validity of alternative responses, develop more elaborate reasoning, and experience patient reflection.

Dimension 4. The teacher asked challenging questions and/or structured challenging tasks suitable for the ability level and preparation of the students.

Thinking occurs only when students are faced with tasks that demand non-routine mental work. Students must be faced with the challenge of using prior knowledge to gain new knowledge, rather than the task of merely retrieving prior knowledge.

Dimension 5. The teacher was a model of thoughtfulness.

To help students become more thoughtful, teachers themselves must model thoughtfulness. Key indicators include showing interest in a student's ideas and in alternative approaches to problems; showing how he or she thought through a problem (rather than only the final answer); and acknowledging the difficulty of gaining a definitive understanding of problematic topics.

Dimension 6. The teacher was a model of thoughtfulness.

The answers to difficult questions are rarely self-evident. Their validity often rests on the quality of explanation or reasons given to support them. Therefore, beyond offering answers, students must also be able to produce explanations and reasons to support their conclusions.

The NCESS research team used the indicators to study several hundred high school social studies classes in 16 schools. Although the level of thoughtfulness in the average social studies classroom left much to be desired, we found that some teachers and some social studies departments were able to achieve consistently high scores on our indicators.

Departments that scored highest distinguished themselves from the lowest scorers by the kind of instructional leadership offered by the department chair and the principal. Although each of the top scoring departments took a different approach to the promotion of thinking, all the department chairs provided programmatic leadership in three ways.

They helped to generate a departmentwide commitment to the promotion of thinking as a central goal. They stimulated and participated in curriculum development aimed at the goal. And, they encouraged a collegial climate for teachers to examine their own teaching practices.

Furthermore, principals in the successful schools supported the work of the department chairs by showing their personal commitment to the instructional goal, by providing resources for staff development, and, in one case, by observing teachers and giving constructive feedback on their efforts to promote thinking.

Barriers do exist to raising the quality of thinking in school classrooms, but our research shows that these barriers are not insurmountable. The task of designing and instituting thoughtful settings beyond the conventional classroom has not yet begun. My personal view is that the best chance for fostering the virtue of thoughtfulness lies in the creation of such new settings.

References

Newmann, F. M. "Higher Order Thinking and Prospects for Classroom Thoughtfulness." In *Student Engagement and Achievement in American High Schools,* edited by F. Newmann. New York: Teachers College Press, in press.

Schrag, F. *Thinking in School and Society.* New York and London: Routledge, 1988.

CHAPTER 4

Using Scaffolds for Teaching Higher Level Cognitive Strategies

Barak Rosenshine and Joseph Guenther

Currently, there is a strong interest in teaching students higher level cognitive strategies. A great deal has been written about the need to teach students to use cognitive strategies in all areas of the curriculum. However, little reliable information is available on how to teach these higher level strategies. Instruction often fails, not because the idea is poor, but because the instruction is inadequate.

There is a wealth of material—as yet untapped—that can provide information on how to teach cognitive strategies. This information can be found in successful experimental studies that have attempted to teach students specific cognitive strategies such as summarizing a passage, generating questions about the material they read, and writing descriptive and argumentative essays. A good number of these studies have appeared since 1984, and there are now a sufficient number to merit using them as a resource. This resource should enable us to develop a richer, more elaborate set of instructional ideas on how to teach cognitive strategies.

The Importance of Scaffolds

A major organizing concept for the teaching/learning of higher order cognitive strategies is the scaffold (Palincsar and Brown, 1984; Paris, Wixson, and Palincsar, 1986; Wood, Bruner, and Ross, 1976) or instructional support (Tobias, 1982). A scaffold is a temporary support provided by the teacher (or another student) to help students bridge the gap between their current abilities and the goal.

A scaffold is temporary and adjustable. It is used to help learners "participate at an ever-increasing level of competence" (Palincsar and Brown, 1984, p.122), and it is gradually withdrawn as the learners become more independent. This use of scaffolds appears to characterize successful instruction in cognitive strategies. Although scaffolds are useful for teaching all skills, they are particularly useful, and often indispensable, for the teaching of less structured or higher order skills.

In the studies we read, various types of scaffolds were used to assist the learner at each stage of learning. During the initial stage, the scaffolds

---

Table 1. Elements for Teaching Skill - Specific Higher Order Skills

1. Preinstructional activities.

   a. Begin instruction within the area where the student will benefit from instruction.
   b. Develop specific scaffolds that help students learn the skill.
   c. Regulate the difficulty by starting with simplified material and gradually increasing the complexity of the task.

2. Present the new skills using:

   a. Modeling of the skill by the teacher
   b. Thinking aloud as choices are made
   c. Anticipating and precorrecting student difficulties.

3. Guide student practice with:

   a. Teacher-led practice
   b. Reciprocal teaching
   c. Provision of cue cards
   d. Use of half-finished examples.

4. Provide for feedback and self-checking.

5. Provide independent practice with new examples.

6. Facilitate application to new examples.

included cognitive facilitators, modeling of the process by the teacher, and thinking aloud. As the students began to practice, the support consisted of prompts, aids, suggestions, guidance from the teacher, and teacher modeling of the task when necessary. As instruction proceeded, other students provided the support.

After students had completed some tasks on their own, the scaffolding provided them with models to which they compared their work (Collins, Brown, and Newman, 1990). In addition, checklists assisted students in developing a critical eye toward their work. Throughout this process, there was a gradual decrease in scaffolding as the students became more proficient.

This chapter will expand upon the initial conception of scaffolded instruction by providing specific examples at each stage of the learning process. Examples are drawn from successful studies that have taught the implicit skills of question generation, summarizing, and test taking. As the reader will see, the concept of instructional support and scaffolding can also apply to the teaching of explicit skills and serve to enhance the teaching of these skills.

Research Basis

Six major instructional elements appear in successful studies (see Table 1) that may provide a tentative model for teaching higher level cognitive strategies. Each of these elements is described below.

1. Preinstructional activities.

Three activities need to take place before instruction: determining whether the material is within the learners' abilities, developing cognitive facilitators, and selecting appropriate materials. Each of these is explained below.

■ Determining whether the skill lies within the learners' zone of proximal development.

A major limitation that must be kept in mind is that scaffolds only apply within the student's "zone of proximal development" (Vygotsky, 1978; Palincsar and Brown, 1984), the area in which the student cannot proceed by herself, but can do so when guided by a teacher using these supports. The zone of proximal development means that a teacher will not be successful if he or she tries to teach material for which students do not have the necessary background knowledge. Thus, a teacher must first assess whether the student has the background knowledge to profit from the instruction.

■ Developing specific scaffolds (cognitive facilitators) that students use to help learn the skill.

Cognitive strategies cannot provide students with all the steps they must master with such explicit skills as long division or writing bibliographic cards. Instead, when teaching cognitive strategies, the investigators (Scardamalia and Bereiter, 1985) developed and taught cognitive facilitators—heuristics or clues that support the learner during the early stages of learning the strategies. Cognitive facilitators are suggestions specific to a skill that help students bridge or scaffold the gap between their abilities and the task. Different cognitive facilitators were used with different skills.

In some of the studies, students were taught the comprehension-fostering skill of generating questions after they had read a paragraph or a passage. (This skill provided students with "question words"—who, what, where, why, how—that they used as prompts to help them generate questions.

For another cognitive strategy, the ability to summarize a paragraph, students were taught to use the following procedures:

■ Identify the topic

■ Write two or three words that reflect the topic

■ Use these words as a prompt to figure out the main idea of the paragraph (Baumann, 1984)

■ Select two details that elaborate on the main idea and are important to remember

■ Write two or three sentences that best incorporate these important ideas (Taylor and Frye, 1988).

In the area of writing, Englert and Raphael (1989) provided Plan Sheets that cued students to consider their audience ("Who am I writing for?" "Why am I writing this?"), and Organize Sheets to help them organize their ideas into categories (How can I group these ideas?" "What is being explained?" "What are the steps?").

For the content area of physics (Larkin and Reif, 1976) helped college physics students solve problems in mechanics by providing facilitators to help them generate theoretical descriptions of problems in mechanics.

A variety of cognitive facilitators or specific scaffolds have been developed and used successfully for teaching cognitive strategies. No rules exist, as yet, for developing cognitive facilitators, but the reader is encouraged to use these examples to develop his or her own facilitators.

- Regulating the difficulty by starting with simplified materials and gradually increasing the complexity of the task, and/or teaching each step separately.

Many investigators regulated the difficulty of the tasks by beginning with simpler problems and then gradually increasing the difficulty. The purpose was to enable the learner to begin at an appropriate level.

For example, in a study by Palincsar (1987) where students were taught to generate questions, the class began with questions about a single sentence. The teacher first modeled how to generate questions and followed this with student practice. After this initial practice, the complexity was increased to generating questions about a paragraph. Finally, the teacher modeled and the class practiced generating questions after reading an entire passage.

Another way of regulating the level of difficulty is to teach only one part of a cognitive facilitator and provide for student practice on that part. In a study by Blaha (1979), for example, only one part of the strategy for summarizing was taught at a time. The teacher first explained and modeled identifying the topic of a paragraph and provided for student practice on new paragraphs. Then she taught the concept of the main idea and students practiced finding both the topic and the main idea. Next, she taught students to identify the supporting details, and students practiced all three steps of the strategy.

2. Teacher activities for presenting the cognitive strategies included modeling the process, thinking aloud as choices were made, and anticipating and precorrecting student difficulties.

Modeling of the steps and the thought processes is important for all instruction, but modeling is particularly important for teaching strategies when many of the steps are hidden from the learner. This modeling of cognitive facilitators takes place as the teacher provides examples. In these studies, many teachers modeled the use of the specific scaffolds by working examples.

For example, when teaching students to generate questions, the teacher modeled the use of the specific scaffolds for generating questions. When teaching students to write a summary, the teacher modeled each step: identifying the details, using the details to form a main idea, and stating the details in the summary. This modeling was usually done in small steps, with each step followed by student practice.

Another form of modeling, thinking aloud, also appeared in some studies. Thinking aloud is modeling the thought processes as one applies the strategy. When teaching students to generate questions, for example, the teacher might model the thought process of starting with a question word such as "How" or "Why." Or, when teaching the strategy of summarization, the teacher might think aloud as the topics are selected and then use the topics to generate a summary sentence.

Modeling and thinking aloud were also used for a mathematics study in which the teacher went through the steps in solving mathematical problems (Schoenfeld, 1985). Thinking aloud by the teacher is particularly useful for novice learners because such expert thinking is usually hidden from the student. Indeed, identifying the hidden strategies of experts to make them available to learners has become a focus of research (Collins, Brown, and Newman, 1990).

In many of these studies, the teacher also anticipated and discussed potential student errors. For example, errors in summarizing were anticipated by presenting a summary with a poorly written topic sentence and asking students to identify the problem. In another study, the teacher showed questions that were inappropriate because they focused on a minor detail, and asked students to state why they were inappropriate.

Or, the teacher showed questions that were too broad to be answered from the text and asked students to decide why these questions were inappropriate. In another example, the teacher showed correct and incorrect summaries and discussed the problem in the incorrect summary. Developing these kinds of examples requires considerable teacher experience and expertise.

The technique of anticipating student errors was also a hallmark of expert teaching in mathematics (Leinhardt, 1986; Borko and Livingston, 1989). These teachers observed that, "With experience, you can pinpoint mistakes students make ahead of time. The more you teach, the more you realize where the pitfalls are." (Borko and Livingston, 1990, p. 490.)

3. Teachers guided student practice as they attempted new examples and problems.

Guided practice, a term that originated in the teaching of well-structured skills, also applies to the teaching of cognitive strategies. For cognitive strategies, this guidance consists of giving hints, giving reminders of the facilitators, giving reminders of what was overlooked, and giving suggestions about how something could be improved.

During guided practice, the students participated by giving answers and deciding on the correctness of other students' answers. For the strategy of summarizing, for example, the teacher modeled the steps of deleting redundant sentences, presented another paragraph, and had students signal when they heard a redundant sentence. When learning to summarize, students would list details that supported a topic and decide which were the most important details.

Students were called upon to justify their procedures, when appropriate, by explaining their thinking. By this process, students' "oversimplified and naive conceptions are revealed," (Brown and Campione, 1986). This dialog may also aid understanding.

As Brown and Campione (1986) write, "Understanding is more likely to occur when a student is required to explain, elaborate, or defend his or her position to others; the burden of explanation is often the push needed to make him or her evaluate, integrate, and elaborate knowledge in new ways."

■ *Reciprocal teaching.* In some studies, guided practice took place in the context of a dialog between teacher and students known as reciprocal teaching (Palincsar and Brown, 1984). Students and teacher rotated in the role of teacher. This practice shifted responsibility to students and gradually internalized the skills.

■ *Work in small groups.* In some studies, notably those conducted with high school and college students, the students practiced the task in small groups without the teacher. King (1989, 1990) reported that after hearing a lecture, students met in small groups and practiced generating questions about the lecture.

This small-group practice also occurred in reciprocal teaching; students first worked with the teacher, and then practiced in small groups without the teacher. A study by Nolte and Singer (1985) found movement toward independence in these groups. In this study, students first spent three days in groups of five to six, three days in pairs, and then alone.

■ *Cue cards.* During guided practice in some of these studies, students were provided with cards containing the facilitators they had been taught. An example of this scaffold appears in the study by Billingsley and Wildman (1988), who gave students a list of question words to use during their practice sessions. Singer and Donlon (1982) used a list of the five-story grammar elements (i.e., leading character, goal, obstacles, outcomes, theme) for the story they were teaching. Wong and Jones (1982) gave each student a cue card which listed the steps to consider in writing a summary of a paragraph. After the students used the prompts to develop fluency, the cues were removed and they were asked to formulate questions or write summaries without prompts. Cue cards were used in studies at all levels, from third grade through college.

■ *Half-finished examples.* Another way of reducing initial complexity and providing guidance for students was to furnish half-finished examples. In the successful studies by King (1990), students were taught to generate questions about the material they read. King provided the students with "question starters" or half-written questions like the following:

How are _____ and _____ alike?
What is the main idea of _____?
What is a new example of _____?

Later, of course, these supports were withdrawn. These half-finished examples served the same function as scaffolds; that is, they supported the student and reduced the complexity in the early stages of learning.

4. Students were given checklists to use in evaluating their work and guided practice in use of the checklists.

Teachers in a number of studies provided self-checking procedures to aid students in becoming more independent. In teaching students to summarize a passage, for example, Rinehart, Stahl, and Erickson (1986) had them use the following checklist to check their summaries:

- Have I found the overall idea that the passage is about?
- Have I found the most important information that tells me more about the overall idea?
- Have I used any information that is not directly about the main idea?
- Have I used any information more than once?

In some studies, the teacher also modeled the use of the checklist and offered guidance in its use.

Checklists have also been employed in writing programs. They range from ones on punctuation (e.g., "Does every sentence start with a capital?) to those that focus on style elements. For example, students being taught to write explanatory material were also taught to ask, "Did I tell what materials are needed?" "Did I make the steps clear?" (Englert and Raphael, 1989).

Even though checklists were part of these studies, we do not know how useful they were. One might argue that students need a good deal of knowledge and skill in order to know what they don't know. A question such as, "How well did my question link the information together?" will not be much help to students who answer "Poorly." More research is needed on the development and usefulness of checklists.

5. Independent practice with new examples was provided.

All studies provided for extensive and varied independent practice, including consolidation activities for putting all the procedures together. A gradual transfer of responsibility took place. The prompts and supports were diminished, and the teacher's role shifted from coach to that of supportive and sympathetic listener (Palincsar and Brown, 1984). In some studies, the independent practice was followed by discussion of the papers or by having students compare their work with a model developed by the teacher.

6. Students applied the learning to new examples.

The extensive practice with a variety of materials—alone, in groups, or in pairs—had another function, that of decontextualizing the learning. The strategies were freed from their original "bindings" and applied, easily and unconsciously, to different types of reading. More accurately, the readings served to link the strategy to a richer set of contexts, and these contexts then suggested the strategy.

Summary of Findings

This review of the methods used in studies of cognitive strategies in language arts has yielded a number of new instructional procedures that can be added to a teacher's repertoire. These elements enlarge our technical vocabulary and may be useful for improving the teaching of both well-structured skills and cognitive strategies. A general term that might be used for these elements is scaffolds (Palincsar and Brown, 1984; Wood, Bruner, and Ross, 1976) in that these variables support student learning.

This research suggests nine instructional support strategies. They are:

■ Presentational Variables
1. Provide specific scaffolds
2. Regulate the difficulty
3. Model use of the facilitator
4. Think out loud
5. Anticipate difficult areas

- Guided Practice Variables
  6. Use reciprocal teaching
  7. Provide cue cards
  8. Provide half-finished examples

- Feedback Variable
  9. Provide checklists

Comparison with Direct Instruction/Explicit Teaching

How does the present work compare with the direct instruction or explicit teaching model that was presented some years ago (Rosenshine and Stevens, 1986; Rosenshine and Berliner, 1987)? Some major categories of behaviors such as presentation, guided practice, and independent practice appear in both models. It is also interesting to note that all the scaffold variables discussed here can be used to enhance the teaching of explicit or well-structured skills. No conflicts exist. This new research provides help for the teaching of both well-structured and cognitive strategies.

One clear advance in this research is the introduction of a new instructional concept, scaffolding. Scaffolds, and the procedures for instruction in their use, provide suggestions for thinking about how to teach and to help students learn other less-structured, implicit skills. Scaffolds may be useful for teaching self-enhancing skills such as autonomy, independence, and problem solving in specific content areas. Perhaps the strategies in these studies can be applied to the development of many desired but less-structured goals.

This research suggests that there is a continuum from well-structured to cognitive strategies. Some of the elements, such as presenting information in small steps and providing guided practice, are important at all points in the continuum. As one moves from well-structured to cognitive strategies, however, the instructional value increases for providing students with supports and scaffolds—models, facilitators, think-alouds, simplified problems, prompts, and hints—during the presentation and guided practice phases.

The variables in this review are at a middle level of specificity. They support the student but do not specify each step to be taken. There is something appealing about this middle level. It does not have the specificity of behavioral objectives that seem overly demanding to some, nor the lack of instruction that many criticized in discovery learning. Perhaps it is the beginning of a new synthesis.

References

Baumann, J. F. "The Effectiveness of a Direct Instruction Paradigm for Teaching Main Idea Comprehension." *Reading Research Quarterly* 20 (1984): 93–115.

Billingsley, B. S., and Wildman, T. M. "Question Generation and Reading Comprehension." *Learning Disability Research* 4 (1988): 36–44.

Blaha, B. A. "The Effects of Answering Self-Generated Questions on Reading." Doctoral dissertation, Boston University School of Education, 1979.

Borko, H., and Livingston, C. "Cognitions and Improvisation: Developing in Math Instruction by Expert and Novice Teachers." *American Education Research Journal* 26(1989): 473–99.

Brophy, J. E., and Good, T. L. "Teacher Behavior and Student Achievement." In *Handbook of Research on Teaching,* 3d ed., edited by M. C. Wittrock. New York: Macmillan, 1986.

Brown, A. L., and Campione, J. C. "Psychological Theory and the Study of Learning Disabilities." *American Psychologist* 41(1986): 1059–1068.

Collins, A.; Brown, J. S.; and Newman, S. E. "Cognitive Apprenticeship: Teaching the Crafts of Reading, Writing, and Mathematics." In *Knowing, Learning and Instruction: Essays in Honor of Robert Glaser,* edited by L. Resnick. Hillsdale, N.J.: Erlbaum Associates, 1990.

Englert, C. S., and Raphael, T. E. "Developing Successfully Through Cognitive Strategy Instruction," edited by J. J. Brophy. In *Advances in Research in Teaching,* Vol. 1, Newark, N. J.: JAI Press, 1989.

King, A. "Effects of Self-Questioning Training on College Students' Comprehension of Lectures." *Contemporary Educational Psychology* 14(1989): 366–81.

———. "Improving Lecture Comprehension: Effects of a Metacognitive Strategy." *Applied Educational Psychology* 16(1990): 155–58.

Larkin, J. H., and Reif, F. "Analysis and Teaching of a General Skill for Studying Scientific Test." *Journal of Educational Psychology* 68(1976): 431–44.

Leinhardt, G. A. *Math Lessons: A Comparison of Expert and Novice Competence.* Pittsburgh, Pa.: Learning Research and Developing Center, University of Pittsburgh, 1986.

Nolte, R. Y., and Singer, H. "Active Comprehensive Teaching: A Process of Reading Comprehension and Its Effects on Reading Achievement." *The Reading Teacher* 39(1985): 24–31.

Palincsar, A. S. "Collaborating for Collaborative Learning of Text Comprehension." Paper presented at the annual conference of the American Educational Research Association, Washington, D.C., April 1987.

Palincsar, A. S., and Brown, A. L. "Reciprocal Teaching of Comprehension-Fostering and Comprehension-Monitoring Activities." *Cognition and Instruction* 2 (1984): 117–75.

Paris, S. G.; Wixson, K. K.; and Palincsar, A. S. "Instructional Approaches to Reading Comprehension." In *Review of Research in Education,* 13, edited by E. Z. Rothkof. Washington, D.C.: American Educational Research Association, 1986.

Raphael, T. E., and Pearson, P. D. "Increasing Student Awareness of Sources of Information for Answering Questions." *American Educational Research Journal* 22 (1985) 217–37.

Rinehart, S. D.; Stahl S. D.; and Erickson, L. G. "Some Effects of Summarization Training on Reading and Studying." *Reading Research Quarterly* 22 (1986): 422–38.

Rosenshine, B., and Berliner, D., eds. *Explicit Teaching: Talks to Teachers.* New York: Random House, 1987.

Rosenshine, B., and Stevens, R. "Teaching Functions." In *Handbook of Research on Teaching,* 3d ed., edited by M. C. Wittrock. New York: Macmillan, 1986.

Scardamalia, M., and Bereiter, C. "Fostering the Development of Self-Regulation in Children's Knowledge Processing." In *Thinking and Learning Skills: Research and Open Questions,* edited by S. F. Chipman, J. W. Segal, and R. Glaser. Hillsdale, N.J.: Lawrence Erlbaum Associates, 1985.

Schoenfeld, A. *Mathematical Problem Solving.* New York: Academic Press, 1985.

Singer, H., and Donlon, D. "Active Comprehension: Problem-Solving Schema with Question Generation of Complex Short Stories." *Reading Research Quarterly* 17(1982): 166–86.

Taylor, E., and Frye, B. "Skills Pretest: Replacing Unnecessary Skill Activities with Pleasure Reading Comprehension Strategy Instruction." Unpublished manuscript. College of Education, University of Minnesota, 1988.

Tobias, S. "When Do Instructional Methods Make a Difference?" *Educational Researcher* 11(1982): 4–10.

Vygotsky, L. S. *Mind in Society: The Development of Higher Psychological Processes.* Cambridge, Mass.: Harvard University Press, 1979.

Wood, D. J.; Bruner, J. S.; and Ross, G. The Role of Tutoring in Problem Solving." *Journal of Child Psychology and Psychiatry* 17(1976): 89–100.

Wong, Y. L., and Jones, W. "Increasing Metacomprehension in Learning Disabled and Normally Achieving Students Through Self-Questioning Training." *Learning Disability Quarterly* 5(1982): 228–39.

CHAPTER 5

Students as Researchers and Teachers

Ann L. Brown and Joseph C. Campione

School traditions that evolved as means of educating some of our students are ill-matched with the needs of the 21st century, when the demand is to educate all children. Educational practices that generated an educated elite cannot simply be grafted to serve an increasingly diverse and ill-prepared student population. Schools must change, because the clientele of schools is changing.

Not only are the clients of schools changing, but so too are the forms of literacy required to find a place in the work force. Literacy includes more than simple rote acts of reading and calculating. Increasingly, graduates should be able to critically evaluate what they read, express themselves clearly in verbal and written form, understand mathematical procedures, and be comfortable with various forms of technology that can serve as tools for learning.

Although virtually everyone recognizes the need to foster higher order thinking, considerable debate exists about how to achieve this. The first area of controversy concerns whether to teach thinking skills in the context of academic study or as a separate course. Although both can be effective, we favor instruction in the context of regular academic courses.

A second controversy has been provoked by the use of the term "higher order thinking skills" to describe reasoning. Higher order thinking skills are often contrasted with basic skills, leading to the perception that the former are not for all. Younger and more disadvantaged students are held accountable for basic skills, whereas higher order thinking skills are seen as part of upper school curricula or, worse still, as optional extras.

This latter view stems from stage-like theories of development which purport that young children do not have the resources to engage in higher forms of thinking. If there is one thing that recent research in cognitive development has shown, however, it is how far from the truth that notion is. Given a supportive context, very young children seek causes for actions, generate and evaluate explanations of phenomena that interest them, and try to understand new situations by recourse to analogy from earlier experiences. We would argue that these capabilities should be built on and reinforced from the outset of schooling, that thinking and reasoning should be part of the curriculum from the earliest years, and that it should be for all students. For this reason, our work on improving reasoning skills has been primarily with academically at-risk students.

For several years, we have studied the reading comprehension activities of academically marginal children. The decision to target reading as a domain in which to foster critical thinking followed from two pragmatic considerations. First, it is failure in reading that singles out children for labeling and remedial intervention, along with all that entails. If one could "inoculate" students against academic failure by enhancing reading, the result might be that their future academic trajectories would prove more promising.

Second, disadvantaged students, perhaps because of their greater need for basic skills instruction, are more likely to be subjected to practice in disaggregated skills that lack meaning and coherence. Comprehension practice is rarely provided. Given that students cannot perfect what they do not practice, our aim has been to provide that practice.

In this chapter, we will describe the history of our research program on reading to learn in a variety of contexts. We began by considering the traditional reading group as the context of thinking instruction, but became increasingly dissatisfied with this setting as a thinking forum for older students. In our more recent work, we have concentrated on classrooms as communities of learning in which critical thinking is practiced in the service of learning science.

Fostering Reading Comprehension via Reciprocal Teaching

We have been involved for almost a decade in a program of reciprocal teaching for promoting reading comprehension. Although our own work has been conducted with middle school students, many replications have been made with high school and junior college students. Reciprocal teaching is a procedure that features guided practice in applying simple concrete strategies to the task of text comprehension. A teacher and a group of students take turns leading a discussion about material they have read silently.

The learning leader (student or teacher) begins the discussion by asking a question and ends by summarizing the gist of what has been learned. In the face of disagreement or misunderstanding, the group rereads and discusses possible questions and summary statements until it reaches consensus.

Questioning provides the impetus for discussion. Summarizing at the end of a period of discussion helps students establish where they are, in preparation for tackling a new segment of text. Attempts to clarify any comprehension problems that might arise occur opportunistically when someone misunderstands, or does not know the meaning of a concept, word, phrase, etc. Finally, the leader asks for predictions about future content if this is appropriate.

The cooperative nature of the procedure is an essential feature. The group is responsible for understanding and evaluating the text. All members of the group, in turn, serve as learning leaders (the ones responsible for guiding the dialog) and as learning listeners (whose job is to encourage the discussion leader to explain the content and help resolve misunderstandings). The reciprocal nature of the procedure forces student engagement; and teacher modeling provides examples of expert performance.

The reciprocal teaching program has been used successfully as a reading comprehension intervention by average classroom teachers with academically at-risk elementary and middle level children. For example, between 1981 and 1987, 287 junior high school students and 366 first to third grade children took part in reading and listening comprehension experiments. The teachers worked with small groups. (The ideal group size is six, but teachers have handled much larger groups.)

Students enter the studies scoring approximately 30 percent correct on independent tests of text comprehension, and we count as successful any student who achieves an independent score of 75–80 percent correct on five successive tests. With this criterion, approximately 80 percent of the students in both age groups were judged to be successful. Furthermore, students maintained their independent mastery for up to a year after instruction ceases.

The reciprocal teaching procedure provides students with widely applicable thinking tools. Perhaps the most dramatic indication of the effects of reciprocal teaching is the extent to which the students improved in settings other than those we control. We have repeatedly found three types of learning transfer: unprompted generalization to content area classroom settings; improved performance on post-tests that tap the trained strategies; and substantial improvement (an average of two years) in standardized test scores. The program now is in widespread use nationally.

Reciprocal Teaching of Coherent Content

In the majority of our work on reciprocal teaching of reading comprehension, we have followed the typical "reading group" practice. Each day, students read a text that is unrelated to the previous texts. Passage follows passage with no coherent link between them, allowing little opportunity for cumulative reference, little opportunity for learning. The students are learning to read rather than reading to learn. And this is the main agenda of reading group activities.

In contrast, learning about history or science demands reading of coherent content that builds successively on prior reading. This enables students to accumulate progressively richer knowledge and to apply principles of learning based on analogy, example, explanation, and plausible reasoning.

We have found that the seemingly minor modification of introducing connected texts that concentrate on an organizing theme has improved student performance in reciprocal teaching. Reciprocal teaching featuring organized materials enables students both to learn a body of coherent, usable content, and to develop a repertoire of strategies that will enable them to learn additional content on their own. Our next step was to embed reciprocal teaching in science classes.

Reciprocal Teaching in the Science Class

Discussion: *Kelp Keeps Everybody Happy*

Student 1:   Why do scientists think most of the sea otters will die?

Student 2:   Because they live mostly in that section. So when the oil gets on their fur, they'll sink or get too cold. And it gets in their stomachs where they try to lick themselves clean—or drown or something.

Student 3:   (*Clarification*) We're missing the boring old chain stuff.

Student 1:   We're getting there.

Student 4:   (*Explanation*) Oil kills otters, otters eat sea urchins, sea urchins eat kelp. Kelp keeps everyone happy. Take out otters, and you've got one of those broken links. Too many of some—not enough of another.

Student 2:   (*Clarification*) Another problem, it says here, is the oil on top of the water makes it dark. It's dark, and the sun can't get in, so it doesn't grow.—What doesn't grow?

Student 3:   (*Summary*) The plankton is hurt because it has no sun for energy, so the shrimp's not fed and the tuna's not fed, because it eats the shrimp, and so on in a circle—or a web?

Student 1:   (*Prediction*) I predict that all of the otters and other sea life will be endangered if this goes on.

The above is a typical discussion between four sixth graders discussing material they have prepared about the *Exxon Valdez* oil spill in a reciprocal teaching period in their environmental science class.

The reason we choose to look at higher order thinking in the context of science education is that science plays a very minor part in elementary school and junior high, too often displaced by extra practice in basic skills. Indeed, relatively few students receive adequate scientific education even in high school, and those most poorly served are women and minorities. Somehow, schools convey the message that mathematics and science are "white male" domains, and interest in these areas among other groups declines during the middle level.

Even when science is introduced in middle level and high school, the emphasis is on breadth, rather than depth, of knowledge. Students are exposed to a wide array of facts and definitions without the opportunity to explore a theme in depth, or to consider the relationships among the bits and pieces to which they are exposed. Even innovative science curricula are often transformed into "hands-on" activities requiring little thought.

In addition, there is an almost slavish concentration on observational checks and balances, rather than consideration of alternate theoretical points of view and different perspectives. The consequence is a lack of opportunity to practice critical thinking and reasoning skills, along with a faulty notion of what science is.

To alleviate these problems, we set out to design a curriculum for sixth to eighth graders that would expose the students to science without over-simplifying the material until it was intellectually empty. We also assumed that in the process, the students would increase their reading, writing, and thinking skills. One cannot think critically in a vacuum. Coherent scientific inquiry provides a fertile ground for promoting literacy skills in general.

We developed a year-long environmental science curriculum based on the underlying themes of interdependence and adaptation. Although we wanted depth over breadth in coverage, we did not want to introduce bio-chemical substrata to children this young. Instead, the students were invited into the world of the nineteenth century naturalist to do library research, conduct hands-on experiments, participate in field trips, and engage in various forms of data collection and analysis around central repeating themes. Central themes included the notions of balance, change, adaptation, competition and cooperation, species and populations, and predator/prey relations that are central to an understanding of ecosystems.

The course includes three main units, each with five subunits, to support collaborative learning activities: changing populations (extinct, endangered, artificial, assisted, and urbanized); food (producing, consuming, recycling, distributing, and energy exchange); survival (reproduction, defense mechanisms, protection from the elements, ecological niches, and communities).

The Collaborative Classroom

Although the topic and themes were provided by us, the students were responsible for doing their own research within those guidelines. They worked in cooperative groups based on the Jigsaw method. Students formed five research groups, each assigned responsibility for one of five subtopics of each content area unit. They prepared books on their research areas using HyperCard and Microsoft Word. Next, they regrouped into learning groups where one member of each group was an expert on one-fifth of the material. This expert guided reciprocal teaching seminars on that material.

In these classrooms, students were involved in extensive reading to research their topics; writing and revision to produce booklets from which to teach as well as to publish in class books covering the entire topic; and computer use to publish, illustrate, and edit their booklets. They were reading, writing, and using computers in the service of learning.

Technology

These classrooms had the support of sophisticated, state-of-the-art technology, including computers and video materials. But two important points must be made. The technology is nice but not necessary. It relies on commercially produced and stable software capable of running on relatively inexpensive machines.

It was designed to simplify student access to research materials, including books, magazines, videotapes, and videodiscs; support writing, illustrating, and revising texts; allow for data storage and management; and enable easy communication within and beyond the classroom. (For details, see Brown and Campione, in press.)

The collaborative research classroom was successful on many fronts. First, as with studies concerned directly with reading, reading comprehension improved in both poor and average readers. Similarly, student writing improved dramatically. In fact, comparing the changes in our best students over a year, we estimate that they progressed from poor grade school levels to using organizational structures more typical of young adults.

The students also showed substantial gains on short-answer questions covering their knowledge of the curricular content. Research students outperformed comparison groups with equal exposure to the material. In tests of application and transfer, the research students most clearly outperformed control groups, demonstrating their ability to apply biological principles to novel tasks such as creating an animal to fit a habitat or designing a self-sufficient space station.

In general, both in terms of in-depth analyses of on-line processes (dialogs, planning, designing instruction) and outcome measures of basic literacy, the collaborative research classroom was successful. The improvement in reading and writing scores when the activities were practiced in learning scientific content is particularly important, given the reluctance of administrators to permit "too much science" in the early grades because of the need to improve reading scores. Such activities contribute to, rather than detract from, the acquisition of basic literacy.

Open-Ended Tests

Currently, considerable interest exists in the development and use of alternative forms of assessment. One of our goals in designing a learning environment was to provide opportunities for in-depth assessment of students' reasoning. And, in fact, the collaborative classroom does provide multiple sources of such assessments as an automatic byproduct of typical student activities.

For example, we can evaluate students' scientific inquiry skills as they plan and carry out actual experiments. We can assess students' scientific conceptions/misconceptions, explanations, causal reasoning, use of analogy, etc., as they endeavor to teach their peers. We have notes and comments students make about each other's work. We can analyze the initial and revised books that students use to buttress their teaching.

Over time, students build up a portfolio of their laboratory and writing efforts. They are asked to identify what they see as their best work and submit it for evaluation and publication. The environment generates multiple sources of assessment, the majority of which are produced by students, not as responses to set tests, but as automatic consequence of their participation in the classroom community.

A Community of Learners

Asking students to form a research community in which they are responsible for their own and others' learning encouraged them to feel a sense of ownership for the knowledge they were acquiring. Within these communities, reading, writing, and thinking took place in the service of a recognized goal: learning and helping others to learn about a topic that deeply concerned them.

To illustrate how these collaborative learning classrooms diverge from traditional practice, let us conclude by comparing them with what happens in the traditional reading group. In a reading group, teachers assign the text; they dole reading tasks out in small pieces; and students must read on demand.

This is in sharp contrast to how literate adults read. So too, this practice is in contrast to our collaborative learning environment, where children read in order to write the texts, working at their own pace, with extended involvement in personally chosen projects.

Another strange aspect of reading lessons is that students usually read in order to prove to the teacher that they have read; to answer questions posed by the teacher, who already knows the answer. The teacher is also the primary consumer of any written products. But in our classroom, students read in order to understand, communicate, teach, write, persuade, etc. Students answer their own questions and are accountable for the quality of the questions asked.

Teachers do not always know the right answer. The goal is reading, writing, and thinking in the service of learning about something of personal interest. Teaching is on a need to know basis, with experts (be they children or adults) acting as facilitators.

Student expertise is fostered and valued by the community. This contrasts sharply with what usually goes on in reading and in science lessons. These changes result in significant improvements, both in the students' thinking skills and in the content area knowledge about which they are reasoning.

Note: The research reported in this chapter was supported by awards from the James S. McDonnell Foundation, the Andrew W. Mellon Foundation, and the Evelyn Lois Corey Research Fund. Portions were adapted from Brown and Campione (1990), "Communities of Learning and Thinking," in D. Kuhn (ed.), *Contributions to Human Development* 21(1990): 108–25, and from A. L. Brown and J. C. Campione, (in press). Also, "Restructuring Grade School Learning Environments to Promote Scientific Literacy," a paper prepared for the Summer Institute, Council of Chief State School Officers, 1990. For details of reciprocal teaching, see A. L. Brown, and A. S. Palincsar, "Guided Cooperative Learning and Individual Knowledge Acquisition." In *Knowing, Learning, and Instruction: Essays in Honor of Robert Glaser,* edited by L. B. Resnick. Hillsdale, N.J.: Erlbaum Associates (1989).

CHAPTER 6

Diagnosing and Augmenting
Basic Cognitive Skills

Charles A. Letteri

They come to school as if every Monday was their first Monday!" Sound familiar? Everyone concerned with students has experienced the "Monday Morning Syndrome."

Why is it that some students learn the first time through; others require prolonged, repeated coaching; and others never seem to learn at all. We are not speaking here of students with severe learning problems or with genetic deficits, disease, or trauma. On the contrary, students with Monday Morning Syndrome are "regular kids," who come to school each day, on time, with most of their assignments completed. They are not discipline problems. They are reasonably well groomed, and they are cooperative.

These students, regardless of our best efforts, never seem to be able to make it on their own. They require help on a continuous basis. They are never capable of transferring information and skills from one section of the curriculum to the next (even in sequential subjects such as math). These students, along with those who always fail, form the majority in our classes.

What separates these students from those who excel? What distinguishing factors account for a student not able to learn and perform beyond the minimum requirements? Current cognitive-based research demonstrates that one of the most important factors contributing to achievement differences is the profile of cognitive skills that a student brings to academic tasks (Letteri, 1991).

To succeed, a student must possess a repertoire of thinking skills that meet the cognitive demands of learning and performance tasks. Without appropriate cognitive skills, students can never be self-directed and independent in academic tasks.

One means of assessing the salient skill levels of different students is the Cognitive Profile. This Profile is a combination of seven specific, independent, performance measures of cognitive skills found to predict levels of achievement in all areas of academic learning and performance. The NASSP Learning Style Profile also provides group measures of four of these cognitive skills (Keefe et al., 1986).

In this chapter, we will examine the Cognitive Profile as an assessment instrument for diagnosing learning difficulties, its use in designing individualized "Augmentation" (cognitive remediation) programs, and its role in a Cognitive Based Instructional System. In addition, we will examine the Cognitive Based Instructional System as a basis for educating students in the most important and in-demand role of the 21st century: the "Symbol-Analyst" (Reich, 1991).

Learning as a Cognitive Based System

Information about how students learn and perform in academic tasks comes from research on cognitive controls and their effect on the human information processing system. This research describes learning as a cognitive system involving the perception, reception, processing, storage, and retrieval of information by the human brain (Travers, 1982). Because the processing of information by the brain is a system, we must ask some important procedural questions:

■ What structures and operations of the system are required for academic learning and performance?

■ How can a student's ability to monitor, direct, and control the system be assessed?

■ How can a student learn to monitor, direct, and control the system's structures and operations for use in academic learning and performance?

■ How can Cognitive Based Instructional Systems be utilized to address the cognitive requirements of academic learning and performance tasks?

All educators want all students to be able to learn and use information from various subject areas. And yet, for all our efforts, we have students who cannot learn, who are academic failures, and for whose learning problems we have had no profitable answer. Fortunately, however, we can measure, identify, and profile the cognitive skills of these students.

Educators can be trained to analyze student Cognitive Profiles and to intervene directly to remediate the identified deficit. Students can be trained in new learning skill strategies, and in the transfer and application of these skills to learning and performance tasks. This training and transfer program is call Augmentation (Letteri, 1991).

Cognitive Profile Assessment and Augmentation enable teachers to direct instructional efforts at the core of the learning disabilities problem—deficits in the specific cognitive skills required by academic learning and performance tasks. Too many educators assume that all students know how to learn; that they possess the profile of cognitive skills required to process academic information; and that to be successful they only need more motivation, more time on task, more computers, more aides, etc.

Research in cognition clearly demonstrates, however, that learning disabled students lack the basic cognitive skills to monitor, direct, and control their information processing operations in a manner required for learning and performing academic tasks (Letteri, 1980).

Learning: A Cognitive Definition

Learning is an activity of the mind that involves performing specific, directed, and controlled operations on new information that results in it becoming part of the knowledge structure in the student's long-term memory (Letteri, 1988).

Learning is not automatic. It requires sustained and directed effort on the part of the student. For learning to occur, the student must possess the operations and structures needed to learn. Learning problems and disabilities are not necessarily related to the complexity of the subject matter, nor the student's predisposition to that subject. Most learning problems are related to student deficits in the specific cognitive skills required to learn and to use that subject matter. These specific cognitive skills are called cognitive controls.

Cognitive controls play a significant role in determining student success in academic learning and performance. Cognitive controls are basic thinking skills that students can learn, or be trained to use, to monitor and direct the operations of their information processing systems. The result of this control is a processing system that performs in the manner that the student and the academic tasks demand (Letteri, 1991).

Many students do not know how to control their information processing systems (or that control is even possible). Learning and performance, for them, is a chance and happenstance occurrence. These students have great difficulty placing new information, in an integrated and organized fashion, into existing knowledge structures in their long-term memory. Learning is difficult (or impossible) for them because of the disorganized and unstable structure of their existing information.

New information becomes similarly disorganized and unstructured, rendering it useless as the foundation for additional learning or task performance. On the other hand, students who have mastered their cognitive controls have highly organized and accessible structures of knowledge in long-term memory that serve them for additional learning and performing at increasing levels of excellence.

Profiles of Cognitive Control

Research indicates that cognitive controls are the basic thinking skills that separate the excellent learner from the mediocre and disabled learner. Although the general operations of the information processing system are available to all students (though not always used), the cognitive controls must be learned. Students must be made aware of these skills and trained in their performance before they can successfully apply them in learning and performance tasks (Letteri, 1985).

Cognitive control research has identified seven controls that are significantly related to the description and prediction of levels of student academic achievement. Each control has a separate assessment, and the results are plotted on a chart called a Cognitive Profile. Individuals of all ages can be assigned to one of three Profile Types (Letteri, 1980).

■ *Type One Profile:* Students who evidence strength in a majority (four or more) of the controls are always in the top 15–18 percent of

Cognitive Profile Chart 1

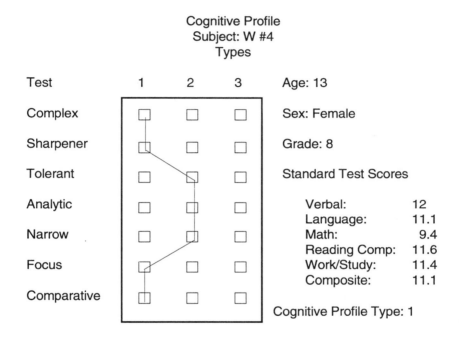

Compu-U-Think   Dr. C. A. Letteri

Cognitive Profile
Subject: W #4
Types

Test	1	2	3	
				Age: 13
Complex	□	□	□	Sex: Female
Sharpener	□	□	□	Grade: 8
Tolerant	□	□	□	Standard Test Scores
Analytic	□	□	□	
Narrow	□	□	□	Verbal: 12
				Language: 11.1
Focus	□	□	□	Math: 9.4
				Reading Comp: 11.6
Comparative	□	□	□	Work/Study: 11.4

Standard Test Scores

Verbal: 12
Language: 11.1
Math: 9.4
Reading Comp: 11.6
Work/Study: 11.4
Composite: 11.1

Cognitive Profile Type: 1

---

the population in academic achievement.

- *Type Two Profile:* Students whose profiles reveal no particular strengths or weaknesses in cognitive control or are highly inconsistent tend to be average (mediocre) in academic achievement. Type Two Students comprise 60–70 percent of the population.

- *Type Three Profile:* Students whose profiles reveal weakness in a majority (four or more) of the controls make up the bottom 15–18 percent of the population in academic achievement. Our research clearly

Cognitive Profile Chart 2

Compu-U-Think   Dr. C. A. Letteri

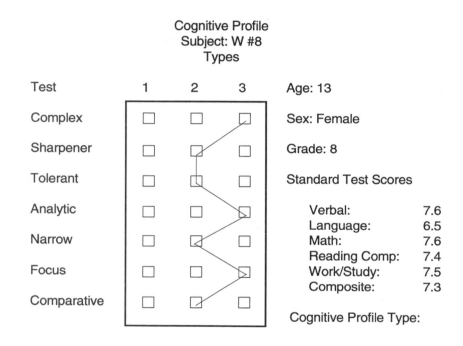

Cognitive Profile
Subject: W #8
Types

Test	1	2	3
Complex			
Sharpener			
Tolerant			
Analytic			
Narrow			
Focus			
Comparative			

Age: 13

Sex: Female

Grade: 8

Standard Test Scores

Verbal:	7.6
Language:	6.5
Math:	7.6
Reading Comp:	7.4
Work/Study:	7.5
Composite:	7.3

Cognitive Profile Type:

indicates that the controls are the major factor in the levels of student academic achievement (Letteri, 1991).

Following is a brief description of each of the seven controls and the skill it measures.

■ *Complex:* Narrow is concerned with the accuracy of adding to and storing information in one category of long-term memory. Complex is concerned with the structure and relationships among all the categories of information in long-term memory and their use in academic learning and performance. This skill is required to view information

Cognitive Profile Chart 3

Compu-U-Think   Dr. C. A. Letteri

Cognitive Profile
Subject: 0193
Types

Test	1	2	3
Complex	☐	☐	☐
Sharpener	☐	☐	☐
Tolerant	☐	☐	☐
Analytic	☐	☐	☐
Narrow	☐	☐	☐
Focus	☐	☐	☐
Comparative	☐	☐	☐

Age: 11

Sex: Male

Grade: 6

Standard Test Scores

Verbal:	4.4
Language:	3.4
Math:	3.5
Reading Comp:	4.9
Work/Study:	—
Composite:	4.2

Cognitive Profile Type: 3

or problems from multiple perspectives.

■ *Sharpening:* The skill required to maintain distinctions between individual concepts and structures of concepts in order to avoid overlapping and confusion among them. Included are the mnemonic systems to structure and maintain information in long-term memory in clear, stable, and accessible formats.

■ *Tolerance:* The skill required to engage and examine apparently ambiguous information for purposes of modifying existing structures of information and to accommodate new information within these related

Cognitive Profile Chart 4

Grade Six Average Standard Scores By Profile Types

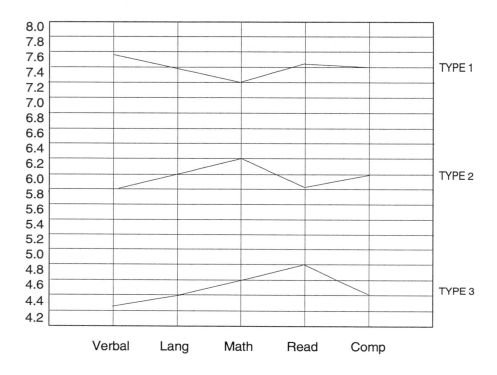

structures. This skill is involved in problem recognition, identification, and solution construction.

- *Analytic:* The skill required to segment complex information into component parts for purposes of identification (naming, labeling), establishing appropriate relationships between the components, and decisions related to further processing.

- *Narrow:* The consistent use of a complete and accurate list of parameters to judge the placement of new information in the structures (categories) of long-term memory.

■ *Focusing:* The skill required to selectively attend to the relevant (important) components of the information or task without being distracted by irrelevant (unimportant) components.

■ *Comparative Analysis:* The skill required to select a correct response or problem solution from among several highly similar but not identical alternatives. The skill to perform a highly accurate and properly ordered and directed comparison between two or more elements of information and to determine and state the basis for similarity and difference.

Each of the cognitive controls can be assessed and trained individually, but in fact, they work in concert during the processing of information. These controls are a part of existing long-term memory. They are used to monitor, direct, and control the flow of information from the perceptual registers (e.g., eye, ear) to placement in relevant structures of long-term memory, and for later recall (or reconstruction) in learning, problem solving, and related performance tasks (Letteri, 1991).

If there is a problem with any of these controls (i.e., Type Two and Type Three students), increments in strength and associated Type changes can be made through individually designed Augmentation and Transfer Programs. Research has demonstrated impressive increments in the academic achievement of students in Augmentation programs (Letteri, 1991).

For example, students having learning problems with mathematics, science, or reading can be helped by specific attention (among others) to the controls of analysis, focusing, and comparative analysis.

■ *Analysis:* Math problems can be segmented to reveal important elements such as symbols (and their definitions), facts, and relationships among these symbols and facts. Maps can be segmented into components such as political borders, navigational symbols, roads, and geographic symbols in order to arrive at place locations and designations. Word problems can be segmented into components to determine the relative importance and the relationship among these components.

■ *Focusing:* In doing math word problems, students often attend to the story first, and then to the math elements. This process distracts students and in many cases causes them to miss elements essential to problem identification or solution. In reading either literature or subject matter, attention must be completely deployed (and monitored) to the scanning of the words, lines, and paragraphs. If attention wanders to a symbol, graph, or picture on the page while this scanning is occurring, the students can miss essential words, or fail to track from one line to another accurately. They can miss words or other symbols essential for comprehension. Comprehension will be inaccurate.

■ *Comparative Analysis:* The comparative process requires that the student first use analysis to identify the elements, and then focusing to identify specific elements to be used in the comparison. The results of the comparative process are statements (rule-relationship) that contain the elements of similarity as well as the elements of difference (distinctive features). These statements become the rules that are applied during subsequent learning or performance tasks to determine category inclusion or accurate identification. These rules are the basis for the construction of problem solutions.

Cognitive Based Instructional Systems (CBIS)

Augmentation and Transfer Programs are designed for individual and small-group remedial instruction. Cognitive Based Instructional Systems are designed for use with a whole class or group of classes, within one or more content areas. Using CBIS, the teacher can analyze the content and determine the cognitive requirements for class success in assigned learning and performance tasks. The teacher can then train the students in the identified skills and how to apply them in the assigned tasks.

These cognitive requirements include the basic cognitive controls as well as more advanced elements of thinking such as concept attainment, concept formation, mnemonics, problem recognition, identification and solution construction, symbol analysis, and manipulation. These cognitive skills are an integral part of even the most elemental learning and performance task.

They are even more important in computer-based learning/performance programs. In fact, computer literacy presupposes these skills and that the student is well practiced in their applications across content area learning and performance tasks.

Cognitive Based Instructional Systems aim to provide students with the most basic, transferable skills a school can offer: the ability to analyze content and problems, and to determine what is required for successful completion of associated tasks. These skills can best be learned through a problem-oriented curriculum, with active student participation in collaborative problem-solving groups. Schools must be restructured to support this kind of cognitive-based learning.

Only the schools can prepare students for the new roles and tasks of a twenty-first century information society. An information society is characterized by ever-increasing, accessible, and manipulative sources of information. Every person at every location and position will have direct access to any kind of information he or she requires. The state of information, its location, its format and access codes, will be available to all individuals. What to do with this information, how to select from the array of information, and how to apply it to a variety of problems must be the concern of the educator (Reich, 1991).

The ability of students to recognize, identify, and solve problems will become increasingly dependent on their ability to manage and manipulate information symbol systems. Students must become "symbol analysts." A symbol analyst knows how to access the meaning of symbols as well as the strategies and operations that make those symbols effective in a variety of task completions, including problem solving. Symbol-analyzers will have direct access to established bodies of knowledge (i.e., facts, codes, formulas, and rules). What will be more valuable, however, will be their capacity to effectively and creatively use the knowledge.

Symbol analysts will solve, identify, and broker problems by manipulating symbols. They will get behind a problem and examine reality from multiple perspectives in an attempt to visualize new solutions. The capacity for discovering patterns and meanings is the essence of the symbol analyst, who simplifies reality into abstract images that can be rearranged, juggled, and experimented with. To become symbol analysts, students must be trained to examine how problems come about, how they are connected to other problems, and how to experiment to discover new solutions (Reich, 1991).

Educating the Symbol Analyst

- *Content:* Training the symbol analyst is now in the hands of a few elite institutions and corporate training programs. The demand for elite symbol analysts is increasing. Cognitive Based Instructional Systems directly address the education needs of symbol analysts through a Problem-Oriented Curriculum.

  In this curriculum, the student is presented with problems involving increasing levels of difficulty and complexity that must be solved through the manipulation and management of information symbols common to a variety of knowledge structures. The teacher trains the student in symbol manipulation and management techniques, as well as in the related cognitive strategies to support successful solutions. Both learning procedures and solution procedures are integrated into the curriculum. Content includes both the information and the strategies and structures required for successful learning and performance.

- *Cognition:* Currrent educational practice delivers content in separate fields such as mathematics, science, history, or literature. But it fails to teach the thinking processes that enable students to use the concepts and methods of those fields, especially in problem-solving tasks (Reich, 1991).

  In other words, current education does not teach the underlying cognitive management and manipulation skills required to identify and solve problems. Teachers must examine content and associated problems to determine the cognitive requirements for learning and using that content. These requirements must then be incorporated into the lesson to ensure that students have both the content and the cognitive skills needed for success.

- *Context:* When Content and Cognition goals are achieved, the Context of the classroom dramatically changes because students have the cognitive skills for learning and using information. The context changes to one of cooperative/shared learning and performance, wherein students work in collaborative teams and the teacher serves as a mentor and coach.

Learning and using information involves various problem-solving situations. In the cognitive-based classroom (or school), the student is no longer isolated and independent, but a part of a team that includes teachers and all other available resources. In addition, learning and performance extend well beyond the confines of the school.

■ *Global Perspective:* If education is to assist students in becoming knowledgeable and contributing members of society, a more global and interdependent view of society must prevail.

It is the function and responsibility of schools to ensure that their graduates have the skills to add value to the global economy, and that this added value will be of the highest quality. Only cognitive-based systems can make this possible. Nothing less will suffice in the twenty-first century.

References

Keefe, J. W.; Monk, J. S.; Letteri, C. A.; Languis, M.; and Dunn, R. *Learning Style Profile.* Reston, Va.: NASSP, 1986.

Letteri, C. A. "Cognitive Profile: Academic Achievement." In *Cognitive Science: Contribution to Educational Practice,* edited by Marlin Languis. Philadelphia, Pa.: Gordron and Breach Publishers, 1991.

———. "Cognitive Profile: Basic Determinant of Academic Achievement." *Journal of Education Research,* 1980.

———. "The NASSP Learning Style Profile and Cognitive Processing." In *Profiling and Utilizing Learning Style,* edited by James W. Keefe. Reston, Va.: NASSP, 1988.

———. "Teaching Students How To Learn." *Theory into Practice,* 1985.

Reich, Robert B. *The Work of Nations: Preserving Ourselves for the 21st Century.* New York: Alfred A. Knopf, 1991.

Travers, R. M. W. *Essentials of Learning.* New York: Macmillan, 1982.

CHAPTER 7

Assessing Higher Order
Thinking for Accountability

Robert H. Ennis

Why should we be interested in the assessment of higher order thinking? The answer is obvious, when we consider some of the functions it can serve:

- Diagnosing the levels of students' higher order thinking

- Giving them feedback about their thinking prowess

- Motivating them to think better

- Informing teachers about the success of their teaching

- Deciding whether a student should enter an educational program

- Doing research about the teaching of and prevalence of higher order thinking

- Holding schools accountable for their degree of success in teaching higher order thinking.

This last function, the accountability function, is a recent arrival on the assessment scene, and deserves special attention.

The accountability movement, along with the reporting of test results in the local newspapers, encourages the teaching of whatever is assessed. Correspondingly, it discourages what is not assessed. Since this relationship also holds for higher order thinking, accountability assessment, even with its strong intuitive appeal, can become an enemy of true education—when the assessment does not incorporate higher order thinking.

In this chapter, I shall assume that accountability assessment is going to be a fact of life for the foreseeable future. I shall not here challenge its use to drive the curriculum, although this is an important issue. Rather, I shall consider ways of dealing with some problems and issues in the assessment of higher order thinking. My discussion will focus on accountability assessment, but is relevant to all the assessment functions listed above.

Strategies and Problems

What can we do to make sure that higher order thinking is not discouraged by the accountability movement? Three assessment strategies come to mind: development, selection, and criticism.

That is: When we are involved in developing accountability assessment, we can deliberately incorporate higher order thinking. When we are involved in selecting assessment procedures from what is available (mostly multiple-choice tests), we can insist that the array incorporate a reasonable amount of higher order thinking. We can examine assessment procedures used for accountability, noting and perhaps challenging those that do not incorporate higher order thinking, and applauding those that do. (The Illinois Critical Thinking Project is engaged in the pursuit of this third strategy.)

But these strategies are not as simple as they sound; problems do exist:

- Higher order thinking is a vague concept with different meanings for different people.

- No matter how it is defined, higher order thinking is not easy to assess.

- There are difficulties in locating good assessment procedures, partly because of the two previously-mentioned problems.

- These difficulties often require that people develop their own assessment—no easy task.

- Disagreement is widespread about whether higher order thinking assessment should be only subject-matter specific.

- Good higher order thinking assessment tends to be time-consuming and expensive.

These problems are not limited to accountability assessment of higher order thinking. They must be faced when we are pursuing any of the strategies mentioned earlier. They can be solved, but solutions will not come easily.

The Meaning of Higher Order Thinking

Bloom's Taxonomy of Cognitive Educational Objectives

One common interpretation of higher order thinking encompasses the upper three levels of Bloom's taxonomy (analysis, synthesis, and evaluation), and possibly the two levels below (comprehension and application). But this taxonomy was not intended by Bloom and his colleagues to be a list of educational objectives. It was intended as a list of categories for classifying educational objectives.

In any case, it is too vague to provide much guidance in designing tests and other assessment procedures. What, for example, is analysis? The word covers too many radically different things, including analysis of the political situation in the Middle East, analysis of a chemical substance, analysis of a word, analysis of an argument, and analysis of the opponent's weaknesses in a basketball game.

What teachable and testable thing do all these activities have in common? None, except the overly vague principle that it is often desirable to break things into parts. Analysis is too topic-specific to serve as an interpretation of higher order thinking if our purpose is to guide the development of assessment procedures (and teaching procedures as well).

Critical Thinking

Another possible interpretation of higher order thinking is critical thinking, an educational goal with a long history, but one that has acquired a strong following within the last 10 years. Again, there are various conceptions of critical thinking. After many years of participation in the critical thinking movement, I have developed this definition: "Reasonable reflective thinking focused on deciding what to believe or do."

Since this definition is as vague as Bloom's taxonomy, it needs elaboration. I have elaborated on it in various other places, including my book,

Critical Thinking (in press), and in "A Taxonomy of Critical Thinking Dispositions and Abilities," in Robert Sternberg and Joan Baron's *Teaching Thinking Skills: Theory and Practice.*

In contrast to some interpretations of critical thinking, my elaboration incorporates creative thinking. It involves identifying and examining one's own assumptions, but also looking at things from others' points of view. It views the actual thinking process holistically, but identifies elements that make up the total process, including these abilities and tendencies:

- To judge the credibility of sources

- To identify conclusions, reasons, and assumptions

- To judge the quality of an argument, including the truth of its reasons and assumptions

- To develop and defend one's position on an issue

- To ask appropriate searching questions, such as "Why?"

- To plan experiments and judge experimental designs

- To define terms in a way appropriate for the context

- To be open-minded

- To try to be well informed about the topic.

Very important elements in this elaboration are the criteria for making the judgments required by the abilities and tendencies. The elaboration and the criteria apply across subject matter areas, but allow for differences between subject matter. The elaboration assumes that knowledge of the subject matter is essential for making a good judgment, but not that full knowledge is a prerequisite for learning about thinking in a subject. Nor is the elaboration overly skeptical, although it does counsel caution.

I offer this definition and elaboration of critical thinking as a reasonable interpretation of higher order thinking. It is specific enough to provide guidance for the development and appraisal of assessment procedures, including tests. Furthermore, it includes many important qualities of people who think well.

My comments henceforth shall assume this interpretation of higher order thinking, but they are also applicable to most interpretations that I have seen. In order to maintain the generality of my comments for those who do not accept my proposed interpretation, I shall continue to refer to higher order thinking, rather than critical thinking, as the quality or set of qualities being assessed. In my listing of published tests, however, I shall use critical thinking as the basis for selection, because specific decisions must be made.

The Difficulty of Assessing Higher Order Thinking

Lack of agreement about the interpretation of higher order thinking (when it exists) does increase the difficulty of assessing it. We need agreement on an interpretation to be able to communicate with each other.

But other difficulties frequently appear, regardless of the operating conception of higher order thinking. The problems are most severe in multiple-choice testing. They give us good reason to be reluctant to use multiple-choice testing exclusively in assessing higher order thinking.

Communication

A basic problem is the difficulty in communicating with students whose vocabularies are limited. In the *Connecticut Cartoon Critical Thinking Test* (presented through a combination of cartoons and reading) my co-authors and I asked fourth graders to identify the conclusion of a very short argument, such as, "We can't clean the park, because there is only one trash can." The conclusion is, "We can't clean the park." But some students do not know this meaning of the word "conclusion."

To them, "conclusion" means the ending or closing off of something, not what a speaker or writer is trying to establish or justify. So they do not understand the question. We had similar difficulties asking them to identify assumptions. Dealing with these misinterpretations requires time and often individual attention, both of which are scarce resources.

Ideology

Another problem is the temptation to impose the ideology of the test author, as in the following Watson-Glaser test item that asks whether *A* is a strong argument for *B*, or a weak argument for *B*:

A. Labor unions have called strikes in a number of important industries.

B. A strong labor party would not promote the general welfare of the people of the United States.

A is keyed "weak argument" in accord with the 1930s liberal ideology of its authors. Even though I agree *A* is a weak reason, keying it as weak seems unfair to some political conservatives with a different ideology.

According to at least some conservatives, strikes in important industries do severe damage to the economy, and would probably be fostered by a strong labor party. Given this ideological stance, *A* is a strong argument for *B*; but a student who marked it would be scored wrong. The solution to this second problem is to avoid multiple-choice questions that call for the application of one's ideology.

Dispositions

A third problem is the apparent difficulty of assessing higher order thinking dispositions with multiple-choice tests. A disposition is a tendency to do something. Two examples of higher order thinking dispositions are the tendency to look at things from others' points of view, and the tendency to seek alternatives.

I have never seen a multiple-choice test that effectively tested for a higher order thinking disposition. Solving problems probably requires using alternatives to multiple-choice tests. Possible alternatives include essay and performance testing, interviews, and naturalistic observation.

Background Beliefs

A fourth problem lies in possible differences between the background factual beliefs of the test taker and the test author. In the *Cornell Critical Thinking Test, Level X,* for example, an item asks students to choose whether a health officer or a soldier is a more reliable source of information about the water supply on a newly discovered planet. It is a factual matter whether health officers or soldiers are generally better informed about such things. The test key assumes that health officers have more expertise, and thus are more credible.

But imagine someone who believes that soldiers generally are better informed about such matters—or that soldiers on such expeditions would be better informed. That person would probably get the item wrong, even though he or she employed the principle for which the item was testing—that expertise and experience tend to make a person more credible as a source of information.

There are several ways of dealing with this background belief problem. One is to interview students to find out their reasons for answering the way they did, to make sure that the test key is not prejudiced against them, and to use the test only with students of the same background bias.

This approach is recommended by Norris and used by him and King in the validation of their *Test on Appraising Observations*. The approach seems valuable, but not easy to implement, and does not guarantee that the problem will not arise, even among supposedly similar students.

A second way of dealing with this problem is to make the test specific to some school subject matter area and to assume that students with background beliefs contrary to those of the author are mistaken and should get the item wrong.

This approach has some value, but it presents at least three problems: it penalizes good thinkers who are misinformed; it assumes that alleged subject matter facts are established and not subject to change; and it will not work for tests that assess whether students can apply their thinking abilities and dispositions in new areas, or those of everyday life.

Thus, for example, it will not work for tests that attempt to assess whether the thinking taught in school transfers to everyday life.

Asking students to justify their multiple-choice answers, perhaps limiting them to one sentence per item, is a third way to deal with the problem. This requested sentence would probably reveal differences in background beliefs for which students should not be penalized, but would require that the test administration include the reading and judging of these sentences. This must be done by flexible people well versed in critical thinking and the topic matter of the item. More about this later.

A fourth way of mitigating background belief is to employ essay testing in which students are asked to defend their answers, proposals, or other conclusions. Such essay testing deals fairly effectively with the background belief problem, because students usually reveal their assumed background beliefs in giving their reasons, and graders can take these beliefs into account. Standardization of scoring, and comparison of individuals and groups are possible with essay testing, but this sort of assessment is generally more expensive than multiple-choice testing, unless the group is small.

Other ways of dealing with the background belief problem include interviews, performances, portfolios, and naturalistic observation. Unfortunately, these are expensive and time-consuming. Because of standardization problems, they are also less amenable to accountability assessment. For some people, this is a strong argument against accountability assessment.

I have used all the above methods and find them to be of some merit.

Locating an Existing Published Test

It is convenient to divide published higher order thinking tests into two groups, those that are explicitly presented as higher order thinking tests, and those that incorporate higher order thinking in tests with other stated purposes.

Explicit Higher Order Thinking Tests

Unfortunately, not many published tests have higher order thinking as their explicit and principal concern. Most are multiple-choice tests. The tests that do exist might possibly be part of an overall accountability battery. None are revised regularly, however, so security could become a problem, especially for the multiple-choice tests. (Perhaps they could be used as models by people developing their own tests.)

The ones known to me are listed alphabetically within categories in Table 1. None are usable in the primary grades. Some are advertised as usable in upper elementary grades, but they must be used with care. Users should be duly suspicious of the results. Perhaps as higher order thinking is more widely taught, and more attention is given to development of instruments for less sophisticated students, these limitations will be extenuated.

Table 1. Some Published Higher Order Thinking Tests

Tests Covering More Than One Aspect of Higher Order Thinking

■ *The California Critical Thinking Skills Test: College Level* (1990), by Peter Facione. The California Academic Press, 217 LaCruz Ave., Millbrae, Calif. 94030.

Aimed at college students, but probably usable with advanced and gifted high school students. Incorporates interpretation, argument analysis and appraisal, deduction, mind bender puzzles, and induction (including rudimentary statistical inference).

■ *Cornell Critical Thinking Test, Level X* (1985), by Robert H. Ennis and Jason Millman. Midwest Publications, P.O. Box 448, Pacific Grove, Calif. 93950.

Aimed at grades 4-14. Sections on induction, credibility, observation, deduction, and assumption identification.

■ *Cornell Critical Thinking Test, Level Z* (1985), by Robert H. Ennis and Jason Millman. Midwest Publications, Pacific Grove, Calif. 93950.

Aimed at advanced or gifted high school students, college students, and adults. Sections on induction, credibility, prediction and experimental planning, fallacies (especially equivocation), deduction, definition, and assumption identification.

■ *The Ennis-Weir Critical Thinking Essay Test* (1985), by Robert H. Ennis and Eric Weir. Midwest Publications, P.O. Box 448, Pacific Grove, Calif. 93950.

Aimed at grades seven–college. Also intended to be used as a teaching model. Incorporates getting the point, seeing the reasons and assumptions, stating one's point, offering good reasons, seeing other possibilities (including other possible explanations), and responding to and avoiding equivocation, irrelevance, circularity, reversal, and an if-then (or other conditional) relationship, overgeneralization, credibility problems, and the use of emotive language to persuade.

■ *Judgment: Deductive Logic and Assumption Recognition* (1971), by Edith Shaffer and Joann Steiger. Instructional Objectives Exchange, P.O. Box 24095, Los Angeles, Calif. 90024.

Aimed at grades 7–12. Developed as a criterion-referenced test, but without specific standards. Includes sections on deduction, assumption identification, and credibility, and distinguishes between emotionally loaded content and other content.

■ *New Jersey Test of Reasoning Skills* (1983), by Virginia Shipman. Institute for the Advancement of Philosophy for Children, Test Division, Montclair State College, Upper Montclair, N.J. 08043.

Aimed at grades 4–college. Incorporates the syllogism (heavily represented), assumption identification, induction, good reasons, and kind and degree.

■ *Ross Test of Higher Cognitive Processes* (1976), by John D. Ross and Catherine M. Ross. Academic Therapy Publications, 20 Commercial Blvd., Novato, Calif. 94947.

Aimed at grades 4–6. Sections on verbal analogies, deduction, assumption identification, word relationships, sentence sequencing, interpreting answers to questions, information sufficiency and relevance in mathematics problems, and analysis of attributes of complex stick figures.

■ *Test of Enquiry Skills* (1979), by Barry J. Fraser. Australian Council for Educational Research Limited, Frederick Street, Hawthorn, Victoria 3122, Australia.

Aimed at Australian grades 7–10 (possibly not the appropriate grade levels in North America). Sections on using reference materials (library usage, index, and table of contents); interpreting and processing information (scales, averages, percentages, proportions, charts and tables, and graphs); and (subject-specific) thinking in science (comprehension of science reading, design of experiments, conclusions, and generalizations).

■ *Test of Inference Ability in Reading Comprehension* (1987), by Linda M. Phillips and Cynthia Patterson. Memorial University, St. John's, Newfoundland, Canada A1B 3X8.

Aimed at grades 6–8. Tests for ability to infer information and interpretations from short passages. Multiple-choice version (by both authors) and constructed response version (by Phillips only).

■ *Watson-Glaser Critical Thinking Appraisal* (1980), by Goodwin Watson and Edward Maynard Glaser. The Psychological Corporation, 555 Academic Court, San Antonio, Tex. 78204.

Aimed at grade 9–adulthood. Sections on induction, assumption identification, deduction, judging whether a conclusion follows beyond a reasonable doubt, and argument evaluation.

Tests Covering Only One Aspect of Higher Order Thinking

■ *Cornell Class Reasoning Test* (1964), by Robert H. Ennis, William L. Gardiner, Richard Morrow, Dieter Paulus, and Lucille Ringel. Illinois Critical Thinking Project, University of Illinois, 1310 S. 6th St., Champaign, Ill. 618200.

Aimed at grades 4–14. Tests for various forms of (deductive) class reasoning.

■ *Logical Reasoning* (1955), by Alfred Hertzka and J. P. Guilford. Sheridan Psychological Services, Inc., P.O. Box 6101, Orange, Calif. 92667.

Aimed at high school and college students and other adults. Tests for facility with class reasoning.

■ *Test on Appraising Observations* (1983), by Stephen P. Norris and Ruth King. Institute for Educational Research and Development, Memorial University, St. John's, Newfoundland, Canada A1B 3X8.

Aimed at grades 7–14. Tests for ability to judge the credibility of observation statements. Multiple-choice and constructed response versions.

Since I am a co-author of some of these tests, my conflict in presenting this listing is obvious. I have tried not to let it interfere with my objectivity, but do urge you to read Arter and Salmon's *Assessing Higher Order Thinking Skills: A Consumer's Guide,* which provides more extensive coverage. I also strongly urge you to take and score yourself on any test that you seriously consider employing.

Since statistical information about tests can be misleading, it is important to make one's own informal judgment about the validity of the content. Do not depend solely on the name given to the test by the author and publisher. Be sure to consider the following questions:

■ Is the test based on a defensible conception of higher order thinking?

■ How comprehensive is its coverage of this conception?

■ Does it seem to do a good job at the level of your students?

Although these questions seem obvious, they are often neglected.

Tests Incorporating Higher Order Thinking

A number of tests that are widely used for "gateway" purposes include significant amounts of higher order thinking. These include the ACT and P-ACT, the LSAT (Law School Admissions Test), the forthcoming MCAT (Medical College Admissions Test), the general (non-subject-specific) GRE (Graduate Record Examination), the Iowa Test of Educational Development, and the College Board's AP (subject-specific Advanced Placement) tests. Of the two most-widely-used gateway tests, the recently-revised ACT incorporates more higher order thinking than the SAT, according to a recent study done at the University of Illinois. Perhaps the forthcoming new SAT will turn the tables.

To my knowledge, most existing heavily-used accountability tests have not been carefully studied for their incorporation of higher order thinking. Cursory inspection of many of them suggests little incorporation. Exceptions are the ACT and the Iowa Test of Educational Development, which do incorporate significant amounts of higher order thinking, and are sometimes used for accountability purposes in high schools.

Most of the gateway tests are used with upper-level students, underscoring the great need for development of standardized, lower-level assessments that incorporate higher order thinking. The existing gateway tests do provide models for the development of broad lower-level tests that assess higher order thinking.

The need is there. If it is expressed in the right places—large school districts, state and federal education departments, foundations, and large-scale testing corporations might respond with an array of lower-level tests, not exclusively devoted to higher order thinking, that incorporate it. I might add that a similar need exists for more tests that have higher order thinking as their primary concern (especially lower-level tests).

Developing Your Own Tests or Assessment Procedures

If published tests do not meet your needs (and for many people they will not), then developing your own tests or other assessment procedures is worth considering. Steve Norris' and my publication, *Evaluating Critical Thinking* (1989), is the basis for the suggestions that follow. Developing high-quality multiple-choice tests of higher order thinking is probably not feasible for most separate schools and small to medium size school districts. The low volume of use would make each test quite expensive to develop. And costs are high for good tests.

So I shall not focus on the development of high-quality, high-volume multiple-choice-only tests. Instead, I shall discuss three alternatives to such testing: one-sentence defenses of multiple-choice items, essay tests with varying amounts of structure, and performance tests of various sorts. These alternatives can be developed by separate schools and small to medium sized school districts. They can also be used by large organizations that are unwilling to accept the disadvantages of multiple-choice testing.

One-Sentence Justifications of Answers to Multiple-Choice Items

One way to counteract the difficulties of multiple-choice tests is to ask for a one sentence defense of a student's answer to each multiple-choice item. This approach necessitates fewer items, given the same amount of testing time, and someone must read the student's defense. This reader must be flexible and well-versed in the topic and in higher order thinking. He or she must be able to figure out the student's background beliefs, and to recognize good thinking, even when the student's actual thinking was not what the test writer had in mind.

The multiple-choice items that form the basis of such assessment must validly test the goals to be assessed, and must be constructed with considerable care. They need not be tried out extensively, however, and refined again and again as is done by professional test publishers. The student's defense of his or her answers provides a safety valve for misinterpretation, insufficiently refined items, and differences in background belief assumptions.

It is even possible that higher order thinking dispositions may be exposed in this one sentence defense strategy, but I have not yet seen a strategy that can ensure this.

Essay Testing

Essay testing, in which students are asked to formulate and defend a position, is a good general way to assess higher order thinking. But how does one do that effectively, and evaluate the results in a reliable manner? I can suggest three often-overlapping methods.

1. Providing considerable structure. One way is to provide a reading passage with certain built-in problems and strengths, to ask students to appraise all or selected parts, and to ask them to defend their appraisals.

The Ennis-Weir Critical Thinking Essay Test exemplifies this approach, and can serve as a model for development of similar tests. It presents students with a letter to an editor of a newspaper that offers and defends a proposal to prohibit local overnight street parking. The letter is in the form of separate numbered paragraphs, most of which contain faulty reasoning (given the test authors' background beliefs and assumptions). Students are asked to appraise the thinking in each paragraph, in the letter as a whole, and to justify their appraisals.

Given such extensive structuring, it is possible to develop a scoring procedure that is fairly specific. (It also must be flexible to account for variations in interpretations and background beliefs.)

High inter-rater agreement can be achieved; the Ennis-Weir, for example, has inter-rater correlations ranging from .82 to .92. Skilled graders average six minutes per student paper, neglecting breaks. But please realize that this grading procedure is more time-consuming and expensive than one that uses a high-volume (multiple-choice) test-scoring machine.

Testing organizations, such as the Educational Testing Service (ETS) of Princeton, N.J., have developed sophisticated procedures for scoring large numbers of essays with reasonable reliability. Manuals for large scale essay test grading are available from ETS.

2. Providing less structure: Requesting an interpretation and defense for a passage as a whole. One less-structured approach presents a more or less complex passage and asks for an interpretation and commentary on its thesis or theses, accompanied by a defense. The student must identify the thesis.

The passage and the accompanying request provide structure, though less structure than provided by the Ennis-Weir, which divides the passage into sections and requests a reaction to each section. College Board AP tests in English and history often use this less-structured approach.

3. Providing only a topic and requesting the defense of a thesis about the topic. Even less structure is provided when a topic or thesis is provided, but no reading passage. The National Assessment of Educational Progress (NAEP) has used this approach.

This is an example: "Take a stand on whether a bike lane should be installed and refute the opposing view." (Note that this particular example provides more structure than just asking students to take and defend a position; it tells them that refuting the opposing view is part of the assignment.)

NAEP has had extensive experience with such testing, so its publications and staff may be of help to any organization trying to develop its own procedures. With the prospective entry of NAEP into state-by-state testing, cooperation with individual schools might be a future possibility. (NAEP is located at Educational Testing Service.)

Another example of this approach can be found in the work of the Illinois Critical Thinking Essay Contest (ICTEC), directed by Steve Tozer of the College of Education at the University of Illinois. In a recent contest, open to all Illinois high school students, the following task was set:

> Bearing in mind that learning takes place outside the classroom as well as in, and that it can be negative as well as positive, what do you believe is the activity or setting that most importantly influences learning for you and the students you know best? Defend your position.

Note that the subject matter of this particular essay comes from the experience of the students, and is not the subject matter of a standard course (in contrast to the topics of the College Board's AP tests). The ICTEC tasks test for transfer of higher order thinking to topics of everyday life, but both school subject topics and general knowledge topics are amenable to the approach.

Performance Testing

Performance testing for higher order thinking is a relatively unexplored area. Performance testing can range from asking students to do set tasks (such as plan an experiment) to totally open-ended observation with anecdotal records. The more open-ended the assessment is, the less amenable it is to standardized reporting, and hence the more difficult and expensive it is to use it in accountability testing. But such open-ended assessment does have much intuitive appeal.

The departments of education of California, Illinois, and New York are currently investigating standardized performance assessment in science. Their performance assessment procedures do include some higher order thinking tasks, but much work remains to be done.

Subject Specificity of Assessment

Should higher order thinking assessment be specific to subject matter areas, or use topics with which students at the grade level can be expected to be familiar (e.g., NAEP's bike lanes, or ICTEC's student learning topic)? This questions is related to, but different from the instructional question: Should higher order thinking instruction be incorporated in existing subject matter instruction, or provided in some general manner, or both? The assessment question is not settled by answering the instructional question.

Regardless of the instructional approach, I believe that we should have and use both subject specific and general content higher order thinking assessment. Assessing a student's ability to think within a school subject is needed, because content has not been learned well unless a student can think in that subject. Assessing general knowledge content is also necessary to determine whether higher order thinking instruction has transferred to everyday life.

The Cost of Higher Order Thinking Assessment

Good higher order thinking assessment is expensive in both time and money. It takes considerable time to develop good multiple-choice tests, and considerable time to appraise non-multiple-choice assessment. Since higher order thinking assessment is inherently expensive, we must be wary of the cost cutter who would shortchange the process.

Another expense is student time. Too much assessment leaves insufficient time for instruction. A related danger lies in what might otherwise be an excellent assessment practice: using teachers to administer and appraise authentic performance assessment.

The problem, as in England's new assessment program, is that most of the students have nothing to do while the teacher is engaged in authentic assessment of small groups. Possible solutions are to cut back on the amount of assessment or to hire people to help the teachers. Again, good higher order thinking assessment is expensive. But can we afford not to do it?

Summary

After noting a variety of reasons for our interest in higher order thinking assessment, I urged various steps to ensure that such assessment not be left out of the current accountability movement. Some of the problems associated with higher order thinking assessment were considered, and a number of comments and suggestions made for dealing with these problems:

1. Although higher order thinking is a vague term, critical thinking, defined as "reasonable and reflective thinking focused on deciding what

to believe or do," can serve as a suitable interpretation when elaborated appropriately.

2. Higher order thinking is difficult to assess, the two greatest problems being variations in students' background factual beliefs, and the difficulty of assessing dispositions, (e.g., openmindedness). These problems are manageable, but probably not within the traditional multiple-choice form of assessment.

3. Explicit higher order thinking tests exist for grades four and up, but there are too few. Tests must still be developed for students below grade four. There are also few tests with other primary purposes that incorporate higher order thinking assessment. In any case, test users must check the validity of the test content for the purposes at hand. (It is unwise to depend solely on the name that the author and publisher have given to the test.)

4. For those developing their own assessment procedures, alternatives to standard multiple-choice testing include requesting justification for answers, using essay questions with varying degrees of structure, and examining actual student performance in some way.

5. Higher order thinking assessment is needed both within subject-matter areas and in the general-knowledge areas of everyday life.

6. Good higher order thinking assessment is time-consuming and expensive.

Suggested Further Reading

Applebee, Arthur N.; Langer, Judith A.; and Mullis, Ina V.S. *The Writing Report Card: Writing Achievement in American Schools.* Princeton, N.J.: National Assessment of Educational Progress of Educational Testing Service, 1986.

Arter, J., and Salmon, J. *Assessing Higher Order Thinking Skills: A Consumer's Guide.* Portland, Oreg.: Northwest Regional Educational Laboratory, 1987.

Educational Testing Service. *Guidelines for Developing and Scoring Free Response Tests.* Princeton, N.J.: Educational Testing Service, 1987.

Ennis, Robert H. "Critical Thinking and the Curriculum." *National Forum* 45 (1985): 28–31.

———. "A Taxonomy of Critical Thinking Dispositions and Abilities." In *Teach-*

ing Thinking Skills: Theory and Practice, edited by Joan Boykoff Baron and Robert J. Sternberg. New York: W.H. Freeman, 1987.

Norris, Stephen P., and Ennis, Robert H. *Evaluating Critical Thinking.* Pacific Grove, Calif.: Midwest Publications, 1989.

Powers, Bert, ed. *Illinois Critical Thinking Annual: Proceedings of the University of Illinois College of Education Critical Thinking Essay Contest.* Champaign, Ill.: University of Illinois College of Education, 1989.

Sternberg, Robert S., and Baron, Joan. *Teaching Thinking Skills: Theory and Practice.* New York: W.H. Freeman, 1987.

Note: I appreciate the suggestions made in preparing this manuscript by Michelle Commeyras, Helen Ennis, Suzanne Faikus, Linda Mabry, Betty Merchant, Sandra Pearse, Nona Prestine, and Philip Zodhiates.

CHAPTER 8

Teaching Thinking:
An Integrated Approach*

Barry K. Beyer

During the past decade, a wide variety of teaching methods and approaches have been proposed for improving student thinking. These range from techniques for teaching selected skills, to specific ways teachers should behave, to general curriculum approaches reminiscent of the discovery teaching of the 1960s. In spite of—perhaps because of—the great diversity of these approaches, educators have too often treated them as competing or mutually exclusive and have directed their efforts at finding the one best approach to implement. But, the truth is, most of these techniques and approaches are not mutually exclusive. In fact, no single approach can, by itself, do what is necessary to improve student thinking to the extent deemed necessary or desirable by experts and observers alike.

Educators who truly wish to improve student thinking can and should combine a number of these approaches. When several are integrated and used throughout a school's curriculum, the resulting program can have a powerful impact. Indeed, the total program impact can be even greater than the results of each of the individual approaches.

Which approaches and/or methods can be combined to produce an effective thinking program? At least five should be considered:

1. Establishing and maintaining a thoughtful learning environment

2. Providing instruction in the skills deemed essential to good thinking

3. Using the techniques and strategies of direct instruction in teaching these thinking skills

---

*Copyright 1991, Barry K. Beyer

4. Modeling by teachers of the thinking behaviors that are supportive of good thinking

5. Integrating these four approaches throughout the curriculum, in all major subjects.

Schools can bring about significant and positive improvements in student thinking by combining these five elements into a cohesive instructional program. This chapter explores the nature of these five elements and their interrelationships. By becoming familiar with these elements and their potential for improving thinking, principals, other administrators, and supervisors can better assist teachers in developing, implementing, and sustaining an instructional program that can significantly improve student thinking and academic achievement.

Establishing a Thoughtful Learning Environment

A thoughtful learning environment is one that promotes and supports higher order student thinking. Such an environment provides an opportunity to think, support in thinking, and engagement in thinking.

By meeting these conditions, educators can create a climate that nurtures thinking beyond the level of recall and translation, as well as a context or environment in which more complex thinking can occur. Such conditions, in effect, provide the "rich surround" that researcher David Perkins, for one, claims is essential to developing thinking.

At least four elements combine to constitute a thoughtful learning environment:

1. A classroom layout that invites thinking. Traditional theater-style seating, where students are arranged in rows, all facing forward, encourages listening, lecturing, and recitation, the hallmarks of receptive learning. Seating students facing each other in groups or clusters, or around a hollow square, not only makes possible but encourages the kind of student-to-student interchanges that stimulate good thinking.

Such a classroom layout is enhanced by means of wall posters and signs presenting helpful hints, suggestions, and ideas related to thinking, as well as generalizations, hypotheses, and the other products of thinking. The resulting classroom arrangement provides opportunities for and invites active student learning and thinking.

2. Classroom interactions that involve information processing, rather than information receiving and repeating. These interactions involve students in posing problems and inventing hypotheses; in comparing, analyzing, and judging the worth of arguments, the accuracy of hypotheses, the adequacy and accuracy of evidence, and the quality of reasons offered in support of claims; and in asking and answering questions.

Students interact with each other as much or more than with a teacher as they continuously seek to locate and verify information, identify other points of view, search for hidden assumptions, and determine a wide variety of alternatives and possible explanations. In a thinking classroom, students dissect, reflect on, and add to what they read, hear, see, or feel to give it new meaning, rather than simply trying to remember the meanings ascribed by textbook authors or other sources.

3. The use of precise, thoughtful language rather than vague terminology or generalizations. Researchers David Olson and Janet Astington, as well as educator Arthur Costa, have stressed the importance of language in supporting and facilitating thinking. Rather than using the word "think" to signify virtually any and all cognitive operations, teachers and students should use more precise terms that accurately signify the mental states or actions to which they are referring.

Instead of saying, "Tell me what would happen next," a teacher or student should say, "Predict what would happen next." Instead of asking, "What do these data tell you?" one would hear, "What conclusions can be drawn from these data?"

Thinking terms, such as hypothesis, argument, evidence, inference, and assumption, for example, not only cue appropriate thinking behavior but also help students differentiate—and store for future use—the essential cognitive operations that constitute thinking and learning.

4. The organization of classroom study and courses around thoughtful questions. Researchers Fred Newmann, Francis Schrag (whose views on thoughtfulness are presented earlier in this book), and Grant Wiggins assert the importance of challenging students to think if we expect them to develop their thinking at all. This means engaging them in thoughtful inquiry.

Such inquiry can be built around questions of fundamental interest to the students and essential to the discipline or subject being studied, questions that also bring students into contact with perspectives other than their own, and questions to which there are no single correct answers or for which there is no single correct way of finding answers.

For example, a question such as, "To what extent did people in the United States cope during the Civil War with interruptions in their personal agendas as we do today?" might well serve to organize a thoughtful analysis of, and learning about, this major period in American history. Structuring student learning around questions like this allows for sustained and in-depth examination of a limited number of topics, continuing involvement in the substance of a subject or discipline, and active mental engagement with subject matter—all of which are required for the development of higher order thinking.

If secondary school students are to improve their thinking, they need a learning environment that allows them to use the kinds of thinking they need to develop, that nurtures and supports such thinking, and that invites them to think.

By attending to these four aspects, principals and teachers can create and maintain such an environment.

Teaching Thinking Skills

Thinking is a skillful (read: skill-*full*) enterprise. Any act of sustained thinking consists of a variety of discrete cognitive operations, or skills, used in various combinations to produce an intended result or product. Thoughtful inquiry, for example, requires, among other things, analyzing data to identify or define a problem; synthesizing hypotheses; recalling or synthesizing plans for testing these hypotheses; recalling and/or locating sources of data; evaluating the relevance, accuracy, and sufficiency of the data found; and drawing conclusions about the validity of the hypotheses being tested. The extent to which individuals are skilled at carrying out each of these or similar operations shapes the quality of the thinking in which they engage and of the products that result.

Thinking skills are, in effect, the tools of thinking. Proficiency in the use of these tools is essential to good thinking. It has been said that if the only tool we are good at using is a hammer, then we are likely to treat every problem as a nail; to resolve it, we just beat on it. But if we are skilled at using a variety of tools, we can select and use those that are appropriate to the types of problems that we encounter, and thus have a better chance of resolving each in the most productive way possible.

Developing proficiency in a number of key thinking skills enables students to cope successfully with a wide variety of thinking challenges. And improved thinking results in significant gains in academic achievement as well as in the quality of one's life.

Unfortunately, most secondary school students are not very proficient in the skills of good thinking. Most of them cannot solve problems, make decisions, or conceptualize very well. Nor are they very skilled at or even inclined to engage in critical thinking, especially in the more difficult critical thinking skills such as detecting bias, identifying point of view, identifying unstated assumptions, or determining the logic of an argument.

Proficiency in these operations is not a result of simply growing older, as experts David Perkins, Robert Sternberg, Arthur Whimbey, Edward deBono, and Benjamin Bloom, among others, have repeatedly pointed out. Nor, as educator Hilda Taba and others showed years ago, does good thinking develop as an incidental result of instruction that focuses exclusively on academic subject matter.

If students are to improve their thinking, school and classroom curricula must treat selected thinking skills as subjects of instruction as important as the course content they have traditionally sought to teach.

Explicit attention must be given to developing student expertise in problem solving, decision making, conceptualizing, and argument making and analysis, as well as to the major operations and dispositions of critical thinking and to significant information processing skills like inductive and deductive reasoning, analysis, synthesis, and evaluation.

Any secondary school curriculum, to be worthwhile, should include mastery of these skills as essential outcomes of instruction. Students must be helped, by instruction in these skills, to take advantage of the opportunities to think provided by a thoughtful learning environment and to achieve more effectively the subject matter learnings that serve as the goals of education.

Using the Techniques and Strategies of Direct Instruction

It takes more than practice or exercise to become proficient in thinking. A thoughtful learning environment and concern about specific thinking skills can prove relatively ineffective in improving student thinking if students are unable to execute the cognitive operations needed to engage in the thinking required of them. Teachers must provide explicit instruction in how to carry out the operations or skills students lack or in which they are less proficient than they should be. This means that schools and teachers should provide direct instruction in these skills. A number of techniques and strategies are well suited to this purpose.

Skill Teaching Techniques

Classroom research recently summarized by Barak Rosenshine and Saul Chapman has demonstrated the value of specific techniques for providing such instruction. Unlike many of the techniques commonly used to "teach" thinking in classrooms (i.e., filling out exercise sheets, asking questions of different levels of difficulty, holding discussions and debates, and even exhorting students to, "Now, think!"), these techniques and strategies do more than simply make students think.

They provide, in varying degrees of explicitness, actual instruction in the rules and procedures by which specific thinking operations can be carried out. Continuing use of these techniques across the curriculum is essential at those points where skills are needed by students to engage successfully in a thoughtful learning experience.

Among the most powerful techniques for providing this instruction are the following, listed in order from the most to the least explicit focus on skill procedures and rules:

1. Modeling
2. Metacognitive reflection
3. Use of procedural checklists
4. Rehearsal
5. Use of graphic organizers
6. Cuing
7. Labeling.

Teachers can use all these techniques to provide instruction on how to perform any thinking skill, in any subject matter, with any student. Some of these techniques involve more than is customarily practiced by most teachers. Space does not permit a thorough explication of each here, but some important points should be highlighted.

1. Modeling consists of more than simply carrying out a skill operation step-by-step as students watch. It also involves explaining exactly what options are available at each step, and why each specific option is selected. Explanation and execution are part of modeling; one without the other is insufficient.

2. Metacognitive reflection engages students in thinking about their own thinking. Helping students reflect on how they execute a specific thinking operation raises their thinking to a level of consciousness that allows them and their teachers to diagnose any procedural problems and enables students to access that operation on demand in the future. It is one way of helping student thinking to become more intentional.

Teachers can guide student metacognitive reflection by asking them, in essence, "What did you do in your mind to complete this task? What did you do first? Why? Next? Why? Next? Why?" and so on. Student responses to the "whats" will be procedures used; to the "whys," rules or heuristics.

In guiding this activity, teachers have students reflect on how they did a thinking task; put what they believe they did into words, either orally or in writing; share their explanations or descriptions of their thinking with others who have engaged in the same task; and listen to others report how they did it.

Repeated metacognitive reflection and analysis help students uncover gaps or errors in their thinking, and acquaint them with different procedures used by others.

3. Procedural checklists assist students in completing a thinking task by allowing them to check off each step or rule or criterion as it is used during the procedure.

4. Rehearsing a procedure or various procedures for thinking before actually doing it helps students recall what they need to do in carrying out a task, and how to structure their execution of the task.

5. *Graphic organizers* require a special note. These visuals are graphs, diagrams, or charts structured to "walk" students through the key steps of a thinking skill, and require them to apply the major rules or criteria of that specific skill or combination of skills.

Not every chart or diagram is a process organizer. Webs, for example, structure the products of thinking but do not structure the thinking processes by which these products are developed.

Teachers can use organizers such as those in Figure 1 to assist students in carrying out tasks requiring selected thinking skills. These organizers, in effect, guide students in doing the skill, and serve as process scaffolds in constructing meaning.

6. *Cuing* consists of using the name or label of a thinking skill in the directions that require its use. Instead of saying, "What do you think caused the water to rise in this experiment?" a teacher can say, "What is your hypothesis about why the water rose this time?" Use of skill names helps students recall what they need to do to answer skill-using questions.

7. *Labeling* is similar to cuing, but occurs after a thinking act has been completed. For example, when a student has reported "It is probably going to rain tomorrow," the teacher might respond, "That's an interesting prediction." Labeling what students do with the name of the skill helps them store in memory what they did for easier retrieval and to use it when the skill is cued in later class activity.

Some of these techniques (modeling, rehearsal, cuing) can immediately precede student use of a thinking skill; others (checklists or graphic organizers) can accompany use of the skill; still others can follow skill use (labeling, metacognitive reflection). All provide the kind of feedback or "feedforward" that actually shows how to carry out the skill, albeit some much more explicitly than others. Each of these techniques, even when used alone, is useful, because it focuses on the procedural attributes of a skill. When used in combination, the instructive power of these techniques is enhanced considerably.

Skill Teaching Strategies

Students benefit from different kinds of instruction, depending on where

Figure 1. Graphic Organizers for Selected Thinking Skills
Classifying

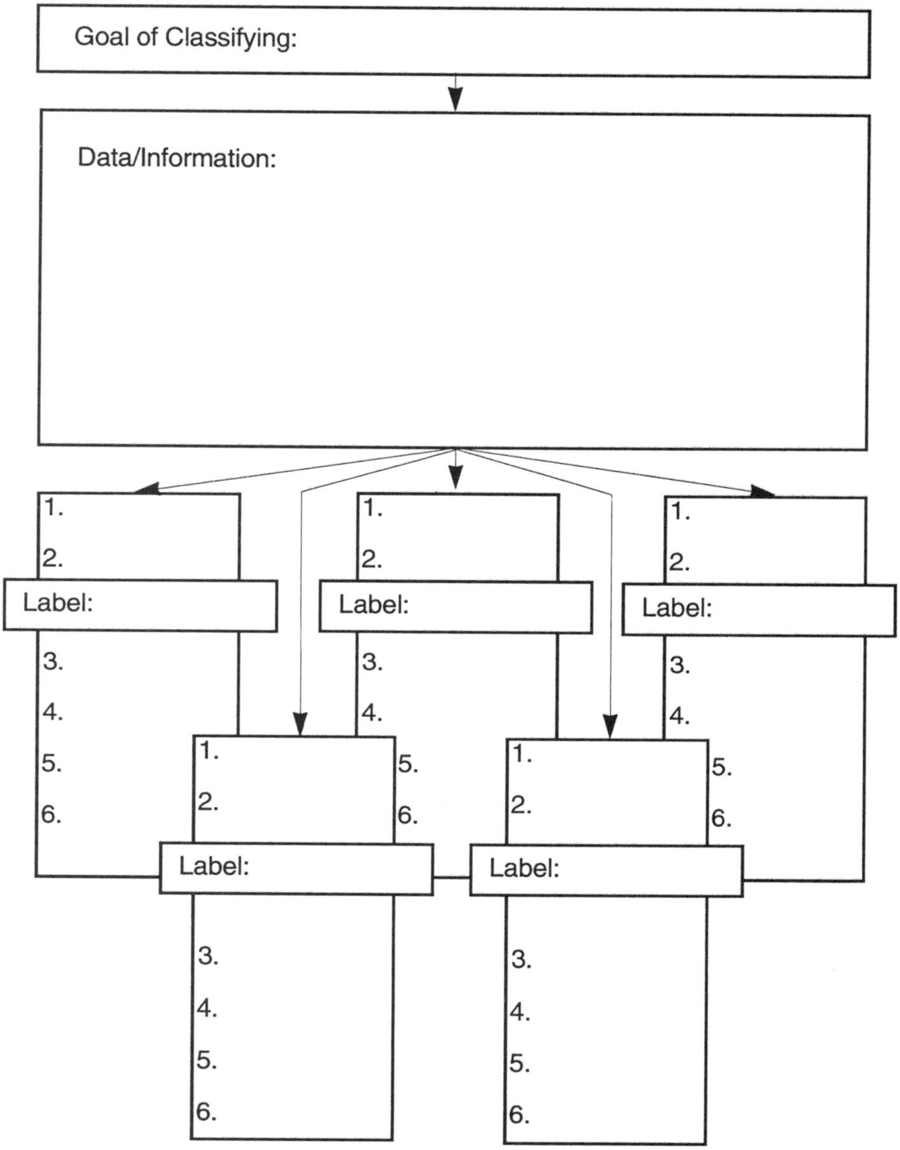

Goal of Classifying:

Data/Information:

1.

2.

Label:

3.

4.

5.

6.

1.

2.

Label:

3.

4.

5.

6.

1.

2.

Label:

3.

4.

5.

6.

1.

2.

Label:

3.

4.

5.

6.

1.

2.

Label:

3.

4.

5.

6.

Analyzing

Goals:		
Clues/Criteria to look for:	Evidence/Examples	Connections
1.		
2.		
3.		
4.		
5.		
Other Possible Clues/Criteria Found:		
6.		
7.		

Decision Making

Situation/Opportunity:						
Problem:			**Goal/Criteria:**			
Alternatives	Consequences/Costs/Etc.					Evaluation
Decision:			**Reasons:**			

Problem Solving

Problem:		
Given information:	Implied information:	Needed information:

My plan:		My work:
1.	——	1.
2.	——	2.
3.	——	3.
4.	——	4.
5.	——	5.
6.	——	6.
7.	——	7.
8.	——	8.
9.	——	9.
10.	——	10.

Solution:	Check:

they are in their learning of a skill. Cognitive research indicates that students encountering a particular skill for the first time need to focus on the skill procedure, not the content to which the skill is being applied.

They must see the skill modeled, and they benefit immensely from reflecting on and articulating how they performed the skill when they had an opportunity to apply it. In practicing a skill to which they have already been introduced, students benefit from reviewing how they did it earlier, and from using a graphic organizer or a checklist to assist them in carrying it out.

Research on skill acquisition and cognition indicates that, for best results in skill learning, teachers should provide the following kinds of lessons for each thinking skill they wish students to master:

- A lesson introducing the skill

- A number of guided practice lessons

- Several lessons that call for the skill upon teacher cue

- A lesson initiating transfer of the skill to a new setting

- Several guided practice lessons using the skill in these new settings

- Repeated opportunities for students to use the skill on their own and in combination with other skills.

The techniques described in the above section can be used in different combinations to structure the various lessons. One strategy for a 25–45 minute lesson introducing a new thinking skill goes as follows:

- The teacher *models* the skill

- The students *apply* the skill

- The students *reflect* on how they carry out the skill (metacognitive reflection)

- This sequence is *repeated* several times.

A strategy for guiding practice in a skill after it has been introduced might consist of combining the following four techniques in this order:

- The teacher *cues* the skill

- Students *rehearse* how to do it

- Students *apply* the skill using a checklist or graphic organizer

- Students *reflect* on how they carried out the skill with the teacher modeling any difficult parts, as necessary.

By hooking different techniques together in various combinations, teachers can magnify their instructional power and provide invaluable insight to students in carrying out any thinking skill. These techniques and strategies may be planned, or used on the spur of the moment when a teacher realizes that students need help in thinking. Many other strategies can be created by combining these techniques with principles of good teaching to provide varying degrees of direct instruction in any thinking skill.*

Teacher Modeling of Skillful Thinking

There is more to thinking than mastery of discrete cognitive skills, heuristics, rules, and other procedural knowledge. Dispositions are equally important. These include a willingness to engage in thinking tasks, to use thinking skills in appropriate combinations, to suspend judgment, to give and seek reasons and evidence in support of a claim, to explore other points of view, and so on.

Good thinkers habitually behave in ways that illustrate and are driven by these dispositions. Improving student thinking requires serious efforts to develop these dispositions while simultaneously teaching the skills needed to act on them with purpose and success.

One way for teachers to help students develop the dispositions of good thinking is to model the very behaviors students should exhibit as good thinkers. Arthur Costa has described a number of techniques teachers can use to lead, and sometimes force, students to exhibit these behav-

---

* See, for example, Barry K. Beyer, *Practical Strategies for the Teaching of Thinking* (Boston: Allyn and Bacon, 1987).

iors—techniques such as wait time, playing devil's advocate, and so on. Teachers also must do what they strive to get students to do.

Teachers, for example, should wait in responding to student questions. Instead of giving instant responses, they should remain silent and ponder a bit before responding; they should reflect aloud on how they are processing data as they frame responses; they should tell the students why a question they have asked is worth asking and answering; they should think aloud as they plan avenues of inquiry; they should encourage students to paraphrase the teacher's reflections and to challenge them; and they should deliberately present and consider information or issues from different perspectives.

Teachers should tell students what they are doing and why. These are the ways good thinkers behave, and everyone in the class—including the teacher—should exhibit these behaviors habitually.

Teaching dispositions, of course, involves more than modeling. Requiring students to exhibit behaviors that reflect given dispositions is also a useful way to accomplish this goal. But modeling is basic, especially if teachers hope to persuade students to alter attitudes and dispositions about thinking formed before they entered the middle and upper grades.

Teaching Thinking Across the Curriculum

Most experts agree that thinking should be taught throughout the school curriculum. Researcher Lauren Resnick and her colleagues argue that certain kinds of thinking may work differently in different disciplines.

Other researchers, including David Perkins and Gavriel Salomon, assert that thinking operations do not transfer easily from one subject or context to another, nor are students inclined to make such transfer unaided. Teaching thinking in a wide variety of subjects assists students in making the transfer needed to generalize their thinking.

Thinking and subject matter are, in fact, inextricably interwoven. Subject matter serves as a vehicle for thinking, and for learning to think better. Thinking and thinking skills are tools for learning subject matter and making meaning out of it. Incorporating the approaches to the teaching of thinking presented here in all or virtually all subjects of a school curriculum will enable students to reap the benefits of better academic achievement and develop the ability and willingness to think more effectively.

Conclusion

No school is likely to make much lasting improvement in student thinking without incorporating the five approaches or elements described here into a comprehensive thinking program. Providing an environment in which thinking is possible is, by itself, not likely to benefit all students. Teaching specific skills without providing meaningful opportunities to use them or developing the disposition to use them well will produce less than satisfactory results.

Actual instruction in how to carry out these essential thinking skills is imperative for students unable to execute them. Teachers who fail to model skillful thinking will undermine the intended effects of both a thoughtful environment and direct instruction in thinking skills. And, unless all these elements are utilized in various subject matter courses during the school years, students will not learn how to think well or use their thinking skills to learn the academic subjects required of them.

By combining these five approaches to teaching thinking, however, educators can maximize their individual effects and produce a program with the potential to make a significant difference in student thinking, school achievement and, in the long run, our civic life as well.

Although the elements of a worthwhile thinking program must be enacted in classrooms, it must be obvious that teachers cannot implement them unaided. Principals, supervisors, and other administrators must assist them in several ways.

First, administrators must be aware of and informed about the nature of each of these approaches and how they can be carried out in the various subject matters. Second, administrators must assist teachers in learning and carrying out these approaches in their own classrooms.

They can provide this assistance in a variety of ways: by formative classroom observation and follow-up analysis with teachers; by assisting or arranging for specialists to assist in lesson planning, curriculum development, and textbook selection; by organizing and supporting training efforts to help teachers learn, practice, and master these approaches; and by securing the materials, time, and other resources needed to implement and maintain an integrated program for teaching thinking.

And finally, administrators and supervisors must provide the continuing support—through resource allocation, training, and evaluation—needed to ensure the purposeful and continued use of these approaches by all teachers. It takes the leadership and support of principals, especially, to bring about the kinds of classroom teaching required to develop the quality of student thinking so much sought after today by employers, university instructors, teachers, and parents. Meeting this challenge is one of the most significant opportunities for instructional leadership facing school leaders today.

CHAPTER 9

The Thinking Cycle

Robert J. Sternberg

Sometimes we view thinking the way we view Trix cereal, as something only for kids. What principal has not observed a teacher trying to teach students to think, while at the same time modeling what is not thoughtful? One is as likely to convince youngsters to stop smoking with a cigarette in one's own hand.

Thinking is for all of us: children, teachers, and administrators. But we often feel frustrated in using the models that are out there, because they are too abstract, too theoretical, too removed from the everyday experiences where we actually need to think. I will propose in this chapter a model that is concrete and usable in everyday experience. I will describe a set of steps that together form the thinking cycle. The steps are easy to use, whether one is a student, teacher, or administrator.

I will illustrate each step of the thinking cycle in some detail with an example from school administration. The example could have come from anywhere, but I like the school administration example for its practical relevance, and because a key principle of teaching for thinking is to illustrate all steps of thinking concretely, in ways that are directly relevant to the life of the learner.

The particular problem illustrated may not be one that a given principal is encountering at any given time, but the type of problem almost certainly is. I have taken steps to camouflage the identities of those involved, other than myself.

Steps of the Thinking Cycle

1. Recognize That a Problem Exists

You cannot solve a problem unless you know that a problem exists. Arguably, the hardest step in the thinking cycle is the recognition that one has a problem. Few people welcome problems, and many find ways of denying their existence—ignoring evidence of a problem, reinterpreting that evidence, communicating signals that it is not acceptable to talk about the problem, and so on.

An effective administrator must actively search out the problems in his or her school. Problems do not go away because we ignore them, they grow worse. What may have started out as a brush fire can become a forest fire by the time we admit that we need someone to put it out.

I worked as a consultant with a school whose new principal recognized the existence of a problem. (He had already accomplished the first step of the thinking cycle.) The problem was that the school seemed dysfunctional, although the principal was not sure why.

Test scores were low and teacher morale was lower; there seemed to be no sense of spirit or educational mission on the part of the staff. The principal wanted to turn the school around, and thought that a consultant might be able to help him do so. He had the backing of the district office, although not of his staff members.

Anyone who has administered a school knows how much easier it is to diagnose what is wrong in someone else's school than in one's own, because people on the inside may have a vested interest in hiding problems from the principal. Thus, the new principal had already taken a significant step in recognizing that something major was wrong, and in seeking whatever resources he could muster to fix it.

2. Define the Nature of the Problem

To solve a problem, you need not only recognize that it exists, but you must also figure out what it is. A tremendous amount of time is wasted solving the wrong problem. People are often ready to rush right in and put out the fire. But different kinds of fires need different kinds of treatments to put them out; chemical fires, for example, often respond better to certain kinds of chemical agents than they do to water.

Good administrators spend time to make sure they know just what the problem is before they try to solve it. They save time that might be spent on false starts, possibly causing more disruption than originally existed.

After talking with many people in the school, and brainstorming with the staff, we concluded that the problem was in the "culture of the school." The previous principal, who had held his post for many years, was an "act your way into thinking" administrator.

He had been lucky. He had managed the school in quiet times characterized by absence of conflict among competing groups, and with little pressure for the school to be competitive with other schools.

The new principal realized that the style of the previous principal would not work for him. Under a new superintendent, there was now great pressure to raise sagging test scores, both in comparison with other schools in the district, and in comparison with other districts.

The previous principal was gone, but the culture of "acting your way into thinking" remained as his legacy, and it simply would not disappear. Organizational cultures do not change easily. When people are accustomed to doing things in a certain way, and have become comfortable with that way of doing things, they will hold on. It is what they know, and they are afraid to contemplate the strange and often threatening unknown.

We had defined the problem. But what resources could we bring to bear to solve it?

3. Decide upon Resource Allocation

A routine occurrence in schools is the discovery, after a plan has been set in motion, that resources do not exist to fully implement the plan. There may not be enough time, or enough money, or enough commitment. If the available resources are not considered in advance, and in particular, if the match between resources and the proposed plan is not carefully considered in advance, the school can find itself having to abandon a wonderful plan. People who helped in the planning are then frustrated because of the lack of follow-through.

In the school consultation, we knew before acting that we needed to know what resources could realistically be brought to bear on the problem. The principal was clearly committed to solving the problem, and was willing to dedicate a series of inservice sessions to solving it.

He was convinced that until the culture of the school changed, nothing else would improve. Even exciting new programs would fail, because no one seemed willing to give the planning time and forethought that would be needed to make them work. The principal had the resources, but what would he do with them? He needed a plan.

4. Formulate a Plan To Solve the Problem

Once you have defined the problem and the resources available, you are ready to contemplate the steps needed to solve it. It is important to have some idea of what these steps are in advance, and to include branching strategies that represent potential contingencies. Of course, no one can guess in advance all contingencies, but it helps to think about them, if only to prepare in advance for the possibility that they may arise.

In the school consultation, it was especially important to plan the steps to take, because the problem itself involved a lack of thoughtful planning on the part of the previous administration, and as a result, for the school as a whole. The school had a bad habit: Do, then think.

We wanted to set a new standard. So we planned a series of inservice meetings at various times that would stress for the entire staff the importance of planning, vision, and commitment to renewal. With our plan ready, we were prepared to act.

5. Begin Implementation of the Plan

The best plans are of little use if they are never implemented. In the consultation, we proceeded to implement the plan we had constructed. We started with inservice sessions and consultations with teachers. But we also knew that sometimes the best-laid plans do not work out as expected. We were ready with the next step in the thinking cycle.

6. Monitor the Implementation of the Plan

Many plans are implemented, but few are monitored. Monitoring means checking right away to see if things are going the way you had hoped they would go, and if not, why not. Moreover, monitoring is something that should be systematic and continual, rather than haphazard and infrequent. You want to keep track of how things are going on a fairly regular basis.

Monitoring is especially important in a system as complex as a school, because one can hardly expect that any plan will go without a hitch. For example, some staff members may actively support the plan, others may ignore it, and still others may actively or passively attempt to sabotage it.

In the school consultation, it quickly became apparent that things were not going as well as we had hoped. We had underestimated the sheer stubbornness of an entrenched school culture.

Some teachers felt threatened by the whole enterprise. They had become comfortable with a certain way of doing things, and were reluctant to change. Other teachers felt that ours was an attempt to load them down with more responsibilities without more compensation. For them, ours was a thinly veiled plot to consume even more of their time, and they already felt that they were devoting more time than they were being compensated for. And still others wanted inservice sessions that would "give them something to do Monday morning."

The type of inservice we were talking about did not seem to them to be immediately useful. From our perspective, of course, their attitude was part of the problem. They wanted activities that were ready to use rather than ones that might require planning. It was clear that the school culture would not change easily. Monitoring indicated that the plan needed revision.

7. Fine-Tune or Revise the Plan

Most plans should be fine-tuned; many must be revised or reconstituted altogether. A plan that is not going well is not necessarily a sign of a failure; rather, it is a hopeful sign—that one recognizes just what is not working, and why.

No one can predict in advance all the things that can go wrong, or even right, with a plan. What one can do is monitor and revise the plan as needed.

The opposition we were encountering made us realize that we had underestimated the amount of resistance we would meet. Good ideas do not necessarily sell themselves, nor do they necessarily seem like good ideas to those whose vested interests are perceived to be threatened. There was surface compliance with the plan by most of the staff, but it was clear that no enthusiasm existed on their part for the change.

And now we come to one of the realities of the thinking cycle: Not only do we affect the contexts in which we work by our plans; they also affect us. Stories are supposed to have happy endings. This one did not—at least, not then. Instead of the principal altering the culture of the school, he was altered by it.

As a new principal, he did not want to antagonize staff members with whom he would have to work. Nor did he believe that change could be imposed upon a staff. Meetings were canceled; implementation plans were delayed. Eventually I resigned, and the principal did not resist.

His solution was to make incremental changes that respected the culture of the school. His was a solution of sorts, but it was one that became the basis for a new problem, or the continuation of an old one.

8. Recognize Today's Solution as Tomorrow's Problem

We often think of the thinking in problem solving as a linear process. It is not. As the title of this chapter states, it is a cycle. Problems in real-life contexts are often difficult to solve. Even when they are solved, we are often not quite done with them.

The solutions to today's problems can become tomorrow's problems. Whatever plan one implements, whatever solution one finds, it will ultimately become the basis for the next problem.

Problems are the normal state of things. No sooner do we solve one than another arises from that solution, no matter how good it may seem to be. The problem may be a very different one; it may be less serious or more serious. But sooner or later, new problems will arise. And our ability to think and to administer will be tested by our skill in handling the new problems as they arise.

About eight months after my resignation, the principal called me. The situation in the school had gotten worse, and he had considered resigning. But then he decided that he was not going to resign without giving things a chance to work. So now we are trying again.

And here is a curious thing: The principal has found that since he started taking more control, the reaction of his staff and his superiors in the central office has gotten better, not worse. He realizes that they sensed weakness and indecision before and exploited it. He is now strong and decided; people are starting to join rather than fight him.

Generality of the Thinking Cycle

I have illustrated the thinking cycle in the context of a school administrative problem. The utility of the cycle is not limited to this kind of problem. It applies to any kind of problem, whether for administrators, teachers, or students. Consider briefly the kind of problem that might be faced by a teacher, and then by a student.

A typical problem faced by a teacher is that of the underachieving student. How can the thinking cycle be brought to bear on such a problem?

The first step in solving the problem is recognizing that there is a problem—that the student is an underachiever. The second step is defining the problem—understanding why underachievement is occurring, so that something can be done about it. Any number of reasons exist—peer pressure, conflict or other problems in the home environment, lack of parental support for school achievement, lack of motivation, laziness, and so on.

To solve the problem, the teacher must know what is causing it. Third, the teacher must contemplate what resources he or she can bring to bear on the problem: how much time does she have, how much support will she get from the school psychologist or other staff, from parents, and from other students? Fourth, the teacher must formulate a plan for solving the problem. If, for example, she attributes the problem to lack of support in the home, she will almost certainly want to arrange for one or more parent-teacher conferences, and possibly for the student to engage in activities with adults who have supportive attitudes toward schoolwork.

Fifth, the teacher must implement the plan; and sixth, monitor that implementation. If the teacher has arranged a variety of supports for the student and the underachievement continues, he must consider either that the cause of the problem was misidentified or that the intervention is not sufficient to change the behavior.

Seventh, the teacher may have to revise the plan, or fine-tune it, perhaps adding more supports, or eliminating ones that have not been effective. Finally, she will need to prepare for future problems.

Once the student starts achieving at the level of his ability, he may discover pressures that are new to him—for better grades to be admitted to a good college, doubts about whether it is worth it, peer pressure to ease up, and so forth. The teacher must be ready for a continuing cycle to deal with new problems as they emerge.

Consider next a very different kind of problem: a student is assigned a term paper. Schools generally do not allow students to recognize problems for themselves. Often, they do not even allow them to define the problems—they tell them exactly what the problems are (e.g., specific test questions, or assigned paper topics). In this case, the student knows she has a problem, and must define its nature.

What will the paper treat? The student must decide in advance how much time to allocate to it, roughly how much research will be needed, and so on. She will then need to plan the paper and then start to write it. She may find that there are not enough sources on the particular topic, or that there are many and that she does not know which ones are worth consulting. Or, she may find the topic too broad or too narrow. The student must fine-tune the choice of topic, or the structure of the paper, or choose another topic altogether.

Conclusion

The thinking needed for successful problem solving is a cycle, not a straight line. The end of the cycle brings us back to the beginning, not necessarily of the same problem, but to a new problem or set of problems.

There is nothing magical about being a good thinker. Anyone can apply the thinking cycle to his or her advantage. It is simply a matter of deciding to do so.

Note: This article was prepared with support from Grant No. R206R00001, Office of Educational Research and Improvement, U.S. Department of Education, supported under the Javits Act. The findings and opinions expressed in this report do not reflect the position or policies of the Office of Educational Research and Improvement or the U.S. Department of Education.

CHAPTER 10

Thinking About the Thinking Movement

James W. Keefe

Teaching for thinking is an important trend. It is not a new movement, as Francis Schrag points out in Chapter 3, but it is gaining in momentum. It is also splintered by two broad perspectives, many approaches, and a lack of agreement about the relationship between basic information processing skills and higher order thinking skills.

In his introduction, Herbert Walberg cited the need to strike a balance among the differing, often opposing, views of teaching for thinking. Barbara Presseisen defined the terms—cognition, metacognition, motivation, content—and the terms of disagreement—content-free approaches versus content-embedded approaches. Robert Marzano further delineated the domains—learning to learn, content thinking, and reasoning.

Several of the authors discussed successful instructional and assessment techniques. Cognitive scaffolds, reflective teaching, cognitive assessment and augmentation, cognitive-based instruction, and performance testing—all facilitate teaching for thinking. Barry Beyer summed it up by urging a comprehensive program across the curriculum, and Robert Sternberg demonstrated the generality of the thinking cycle.

Teaching for thinking can work, then, but teachers and administrators must thoughtfully sort out the ambiguities.

Human Information Processing

Too many students, as Charles Letteri laments, seem to come to school for the first day, each day. Some students think and perform well outside school, yet do poorly in academic subjects. Others exhibit intelligence and the ability to think creatively, but cannot complete daily assignments or participate successfully in classroom activities. Still others do well in ordinary schoolwork but seem unable to engage in higher order thinking. The following continuum of skills or capabilities is implied in these common student behaviors.

Continuum of Information Processing Skills

Cognitive Controls	Learning To Learn	Content Thinking	Reflective Reasoning

| Basic | | | Higher |

This continuum flows from basic thinking skills (e.g., analysis, categorizing, sequential and simultaneous processing) through learning-to-learn (self-management) strategies and content-based thinking, to. higher order forms (e.g., extrapolation, evaluation, critical thinking, creative thinking).

Students may, and probably do, have skills at many places on the continuum. A particular learner, for example, may have strong analytic skills but weak simultaneous processing (visuo-spatial/relational) skills at the cognitive control level, average learning-to-learn skills, poor to fair understanding of various subject contents, and good critical thinking or everyday thinking capabilities. (Everyday thinking is complex and higher order.) The strong analytic skills at the lower order level support and make possible the strengths at the higher levels.

On the other hand, weaknesses at the lower levels can lead to weaknesses at other points in the continuum. Simultaneous processing weakness, for example, can inhibit learning in various content areas (e.g., vocational arts, science) and reduce effectiveness in analogic reasoning (higher order). Weak learning-to-learn management can cripple content thinking and restrict higher order thinking.

If we add the four aspects of thinking suggested by Barbara Presseisen in Chapter 1 to our continuum, we have a simple matrix for thinking about thinking and the thinking movement (See Figure 1).

Figure 1. Thinking Matrix

Levels:	Cognitive Controls	Learning To Learn	Content Thinking	Reflective Reasoning
<u>Aspects</u> Cognition	1	5	9	13
Metacognition	2	6	10	14
Motivation	3	7	11	15
Content Structure	4	8	12	16

Elements of the Thinking Matrix

In recent years, many psychologists have come to view the brain as a very complex system for processing and storing information (Travers, 1982). This conceptualization of human learning as information processing, storage, and use can be very meaningful to educators. The view has been well received in higher education, but as yet has not much influenced elementary and secondary schooling, which still largely emphasize behaviorist approaches.

Most educators view the acquisition of essential knowledge and skills as the primary purpose of schooling. Research on information processing sheds a great deal of light on how knowledge is acquired, stored, and recalled. The process by which the brain systematically collects information is known as perception. Perception, in turn, is related to memory—both storage and recall—and to how each human being develops, organizes knowledge, and uses language.

In Chapter 6, Letteri pointed out that learning is not automatic; it requires sustained and directed effort. In Letteri's view (1991), all content (subject matter) is information, and must pass through the individual's information processing system to be learned, retained, and recalled. After information is received from the external environment through the senses and stored briefly in perceptual memory, the mind makes a decision what to do about a message.

It may reject the information, memorize it for short-term recall, transform it to conform to prior messages, or learn it by integrating, assimilating, differentiating, or associating it in working and long-term memory. Real learning occurs only when the information becomes a part of long-term memory—the individual's cognitive structure is changed. (Memorizing is not the same as learning.)

Effectiveness in thinking is dependent on skill and control in information processing. Effective learning and thinking walk hand in hand. The Thinking Matrix profiles the nature of this relationship in terms of eight elements.

Levels of Thinking

■ The most basic capabilities of the information processing system are called cognitive controls. For learning to occur, the student must possess the needed cognitive skills and structures. Most learning problems are related to specific cognitive skill deficiencies. Fortunately, the cognitive skills (controls) can be improved through training so that virtually every learner can use (and direct) the various operations of learning and thinking. Students improve in all learning and thinking by improving their skills of analysis, selective attention, categorizing, memory, etc.

■ Learning-to-learn strategies are ways that students regulate their information processing. As cognitive control skills are developed, the key to higher levels of thinking is consistent management of these basic skills—controlling the controls. Students learn how to learn in different content areas and under differing learning conditions. They develop skills in transfer—the capability of using knowledge and skills in similar but unfamiliar areas.

■ Content thinking involves using cognitive control and management skills in combination to process subject matter content. Such skills as concept attainment and development, pattern recognition, and synthesizing enable learners to understand and learn new concepts and to comprehend, organize, and integrate new bodies of knowledge.

■ Reflective reasoning moves beyond simple rules, relationships, and principles to higher frameworks of meaning—analogy, extrapolation, evaluation, elaboration, invention. Reasoning skills enable learners to use information to restructure their understanding of various bodies of content. Reasoning is the end product of human information processing—using knowledge to create new and more complex cognitive structures.

Aspects of Thinking

■ Cognition describes the cognitive process itself, the mental acts whereby knowledge is acquired and integrated into an individual's cognitive structure (long-term memory). Cognition entails perceiving, learning, thinking, problem solving, and remembering. It involves different manifestations of intelligence—from verbal and academic abilities, to artistic talents, to social skills.

■ Metacognition is the learner's recognition and regulation of his or her own processes of thinking. Metacognitive skill means that the learner recognizes how and with what degree of capability he or she processes information and is willing to manage and improve it. Metacognition is often called the executive skill, because it implies that the learner has taken charge of his or her own thinking.

- Motivation (or conation) encompasses the attitudinal and emotional aspects of learning. Students learn more readily and better if they like what they are learning. Bloom (1976) has pointed out that students are variously motivated to learn depending on whether they like school, the subject, the teacher, and whether they have previously been successful in a given area of learning.

- Content structure involves epistemological considerations: how a particular subject content influences what is learned; how knowledge is classified; the methods used to define content; and the findings of mature scholars that students must know and use to attain their own, more limited mastery. Transfer of knowledge and skills is at the heart of this aspect of thinking.

Keeping in mind the meaning of the various elements of the Thinking Matrix, it is fairly easy to classify the contributions of our authors. Thoughtful lessons (Chapter 3) are content thinking that emphasizes motivation and the structure of the experience (cells 11 and 12 of the matrix). Scaffolds (Chapter 4) facilitate the presentation of content, guided student practice, and feedback to students. They lie in the middle of the matrix, consisting of learning-to-learn and content thinking strategies that affect all aspects of thinking (cells 5 to 12 of the matrix).

Reciprocal teaching (Chapter 5) can involve any of the cells of the matrix beyond cognitive controls. Like scaffolds, it is primarily concerned with the learning-to-learn and content thinking dimensions. Cognitive augmentation and transfer and cognitive-based instruction (Chapter 6) are concerned with cognitive control, learning-to-learn skills, and content skills in all aspects of thinking (cells 1 to 12).

The integrated approach to thinking proposed by Barry Beyer (Chapter 8) can range across the entire matrix if it is implemented in a comprehensive manner. Robert Sternberg's "thinking cycle" (Chapter 9) is, in the final analysis, a plea for using such a comprehensive plan.

The Thinking Movement

In recent years, many people have claimed that American students cannot think effectively. A whole array of reports, books, and articles has been written supporting or describing programs about thinking. Many of these publications mention students' inability to perform complex academic tasks or to answer higher order questions. The blame is imputed to too much group-oriented instruction, too little teacher-student-peer interaction, and the textbook-to-test teaching methodology of most classrooms.

Contemporary approaches to the teaching of thinking use such terms as critical and creative thinking, thinking processes and skills, metacognitive and memory strategies. In general, all these labels define capabilities that enable individual students to manipulate knowledge and experience in useful and adaptive ways.

Thinking *processes,* for example, include concept and principle formation, comprehension, problem solving and decision making, research and composition skills, and the skills of verbal interaction.

Thinking *skills* exist more at the micro level. (Processes are more complex than skills.) Skills are the building blocks of thinking, such as focusing and defining, gathering information, remembering, organizing and analyzing, generating and integrating new information, etc.

Many of these terms are no more than synonyms for various phases of the human information processing system. Processes such as attention, perception, and memory; and operations such as integration, differentiation, association, and retrieval are internal to the system. Any discussion of improved thinking necessarily implies an understanding and application of information processing theory. The ultimate success of the thinking skills movement, then, will depend almost entirely on the acceptance of an information processing approach to school learning and instruction.

Albert Benderson (1990), in a recent Educational Testing Service publication, *Critical Thinking: Critical Issues,* cites the rift that divides experts in the field as the principal obstacle to progress. He comments:

Both philosophers and psychologists have come to view the teaching of thinking

as their own special skill, but their perspectives are intrinsically different . . . .
Philosophers stress the need for "critical thinking," while psychologists prefer
the term "thinking skills" . . . . In these variations on a theme, the philosophers
stress logic and objective reasoning as the core of critical thinking. The psychologists take a different tack, focusing on the process of thinking itself . . . .
Philosophers are basically interested in the exercise of logic and reason as tools
to elucidate certain fundamental truths . . . . The programs they recommend for
the schools emphasize the development of rational thinking as a tool for making
moral and ethical decisions . . . . Psychologists, on the other hand, are concerned
with the thinking process, and, with respect to education, how that process
develops as children grow . . . . Problem solving is emphasized rather than logic.

We can say similar things about the rift within psychology itself. Some
psychologists concentrate on the thinking process itself, and the skills
and strategies needed to make it work. Others focus on problem solving
as the end project—the higher end of our thinking continuum.

Those who emphasize the process are concerned with cognitive controls
and learning-to-learn strategies. Those who favor the higher end of the
continuum ignore cognitive controls (some seem not to know they exist)
and emphasize the need for higher order skills in life and work.

Of course, everyone is right. With the psychologists, we affirm the need
for both essential information processing skills and higher order problem-
solving skills. With the philosophers, we support critical, rational, and
reflective reasoning.

We would emphasize, however, the importance of essential skills for
school-based learning, the critical need for learning-to-learn skills in both
school and life, and the developmental nature of human information processing. Students need some essential skills to engage in any higher order
thinking.

For truly effective critical and reflective thinking, they need sophisticated control of all essential processing and adequate content knowledge.
In terms of our continuum, they must have functional skills at the lower
levels to achieve consistent skill at the upper levels.

The cognitive trend is probably sufficiently established in contemporary thinking about human intelligence and cognitive/learning style that
it will have a significant influence on the way instruction is planned and
delivered. We may have to wait until the next decade or later for any rec-

ognizable change in the instructional system itself, but cognitive style assessment is already well on the way to becoming a regular element in instructional diagnosis, and higher order thinking proposals dominate the educational policy agenda.

There is a Chinese proverb that says a journey of 1,000 miles begins with the first step. Our next step is to firmly ground our applications of schooling in cognitive science—in a working knowledge of the human information processing system. Educators must know enough about the process of learning and thinking to teach students how to learn and to think. We must come to understand and to involve students in understanding and using their cognitive controls and the powerful higher order strategies for improving their storage, retrieval, and manipulation of information.

Specifically:

1. We must train cognitive specialists (much like our current reading specialists) who will serve as resource teachers, helping classroom teachers identify and enhance the cognitive skills of learners. These specialists must be expert not only in first-level cognitive skill assessment, with instruments like the NASSP *Learning Style Profile,* (Keefe et al., 1986, 1989), but be capable of designing augmentation programs for students with cognitive skill deficiencies. (Colleges and universities will need to develop programs to prepare these specialists.)

2. We must also develop curricula for the major subject fields that are sensitive to the levels of cognitive skill in individual learners and attempt to elicit higher order thinking in the various content domains. Practically speaking, this means designing curricula that use strategies like scaffolds, schemas, semantic maps, and cognitive networks to help students learn and think in meaningful and clearly organized ways. Textbook publishers will need to collaborate both with content authors and cognitive specialists if this goal is to be realized.

Teaching for thinking is a realizable goal. The thinking movement may well be the integrating force that pulls together policy makers, educational practitioners, researchers, parents, and students to really restructure our schools. If this happens, schools may yet become thinking places where students learn to love learning and prepare themselves for truly thoughtful lives.

References

Benderson, A. "Critical Thinking: Critical Issues." *Focus* 24(1990). Princeton, N.J.: Educational Testing Service.

Bloom, B. S. *Human Characteristics and School Learning.* New York: McGraw-Hill, 1976.

Keefe, J. W.; Monk, J. S.; Letteri, C. A.; Languis, M.; and Dunn, R. *NASSP Learning Style Profile.* Reston, Va.: NASSP, 1986, 1989.

Letteri, C. A. "Cognitive Profile: Academic Achievement." In *Cognitive Science: Contribution to Educational Practice,* edited by M. Languis. Philadelphia, Pa.: Gardron and Breach, 1991.

Travers, R. M. W. *Essentials of Learning.* New York: Macmillan, 1982.